HUMANISM AND ETHICS

AN INTRODUCTION TO
HEIDEGGER'S LETTER ON HUMANISM
WITH A
CRITICAL BIBLIOGRAPHY

© 1972 by Nauwelaerts, Louvain.

All rights reserved. No part of this book may be reproduced or translated in any form, by print, photoprint, microfilm, microfiche or any other means without written permission from the publisher.

ROBERT HENRI COUSINEAU

HUMANISM AND ETHICS

AN INTRODUCTION TO
HEIDEGGER'S LETTER ON HUMANISM
WITH A
CRITICAL BIBLIOGRAPHY

ÉDITIONS NAUWELAERTS | BÉATRICE-NAUWELAERTS
2, Place Mgr Ladeuze | 4, Rue de Fleurus
LOUVAIN | PARIS (VIᵉ)

1972

PREFACE

Our exposition and critical study are formally oriented by the ideas of humanism and fundamental ethics as found in Heidegger's *Letter on Humanism*. Though the Letter is one of the shorter and clearest of his writings, it has, because of its import, the greatest variety of radically differing interpretations. Because the Letter recapitulates and projects Heidegger's thought and because any serious consideration of man and *Dasein* becomes the immediate correlate of the philosopher's central question on Being, this critical study cannot but touch the entire spectrum of Heideggerian interpretations.

The theme of humanism and ethics is not only central but also pertinent. An inquiry into the possibility of human action in Heidegger's thought and among philosophers and theologians formally interpreting this thought becomes an inquiry into the positive possibility of responsible behavior where one is actually questioning the nature of the historical rôle left open to man for human accomplishment and personal realization in relation to Being understood either as amorphous or personal, as history or destiny, as present or eschatological. In addition to questioning anew some of the most classic problems, the Letter leads one to the most contemporaneous questions: technicity and man in the modern world, language and structuralism, and the relationship between "dying man" and the so-called death of God.

Apart from the significance and timeliness of this critical study certain important advantages and results accrue from the particular approach employed:

— An exposition of the text of the Letter brings out the salient points, the principal sources of ambiguity and corrects the more important mistakes of translation.

— From this exposition and from the literature, various

types of interpretations arise; these are examined and classified.

— A coded classification is then placed before the critical evaluations of the authors in order to facilitate grouping for further research and analysis.

— By analyzing the basic tendency of an author's interpretation rather than merely the last work to date, the critical bibliography's life-span is enhanced, given the fact that the major turning point of Heidegger's thought has already occurred.

— Only one person has done all the research, reading and analyses in the original languages (Dutch, English, French, German, Italian, Portuguese, Spanish) thus assuring a strict continuity and the possibility for the reader to discover and bracket as a given constant what he may consider to be the author's bias.

— The critical evaluations are rendered more readable not only because of this "subjective" continuity but especially because of the thematic basis which organizes them.

— Heideggerian literature has become so vast that the multiplication of bibliographies no longer makes it manageable. A strictly critical one is needed. Given the wide divergence of interpretations, this work has the not entirely unforeseeable result of being a "de-mythologization" of the literature. Therefore, a special attempt at conciseness and clearness has been made to have a handy, scholarly tool.

R.H.C., s.j.

I
INTRODUCTION

Whoever is somewhat familiar with Heidegger's thought must be impressed by both the great divergence of interpretation and the surprising lack of serious commentary on the meaning and the import of his *Letter on Humanism*, especially if one considers his thought as really pertinent to some of the more decisive philosophical questions of today. This Letter is uniquely pivotal in the development of his thought: it explicitly looks back at previous works to bring out latent interpretations, it takes a firmer stand on some of the more important aspects of his thought and, as we shall indicate, it looks forward to its future explicitation or possibility thereof.

One must recall that Heidegger writes the Letter during the period between the successive additions and changes brought to the text of his *Was ist Metaphysik*? At that time he was rethinking the relationship between time and being, man and manifestation, as well as the entire function of the symbolic and prophetic nature of the poet's task. It was while he was at this crucial turning point that he received a letter asking him when he would write upon the subject of humanism and ethics; thus, we believe that it is most important in analyzing his answer, the Letter before us, to bear in mind that he keeps open the poetic dimension and that it, more than any other single factor, accounts for the orientation and open thrust of his thought and explains, through the failure to recognize the poetic rôle, most of the serious misreadings of the Letter.

As an indication of how the Letter looks forward to Heidegger's later development of the poetic function and of the ever, increasing importance of language, he states that since the act of thinking the truth of Being is at the same time the thinking through of the "humanitas of homo humanus", what matters is that *humanitas* be at the service of the truth of Being.

If we inquire what sort of humanism this would be in reality, then we shall have to look at the behavior exemplified by the poet. Such is the implication of Heidegger's discours on the *ethos* of man. For the meaning of ethos is to dwell, to inhabit, to journey along in the truth, and this as a being-in-the-world. But this type of comportment belongs precisely to the one who dwells poetically on this earth — to paraphrase one of Heidegger's favorite lines from Hölderlin. Man must live in and according to such an ethos. Humanism in its most fundamental sense and in its historical unfolding will be the process of "coming to the word" — to speech, an expression found at the beginning of the Letter as the "engagement par l'Etre".[1] It is likewise the process expressed at the very end of the Letter as announcing the principal themes to be explicitated in the *Unterwegs zur Sprache,* since it relates one's making his way and the event of language: "Die Sprache ist so die Sprache des Seins", for a man in the countryside who makes his way. For us, the main thrust of the Letter leaves open (precisely as that-which-signifies) the ultimate relation between the word and the sacred; in this we have an allusion to Hölderlin's poem: "Wie wenn an Feiertage, das Feld zu sehn / ein Landmann geht...// Und was ich sah, das Heilige sei mein Wort».

We shall, however, limit our formal consideration to Heidegger's notion of "humanism" and "ethics". But on what ground may we do so? On one more solid, perhaps, than Heidegger's who, as we shall see shortly, marks off a limit to his own philosophy. We set in fact no arbitrary limit in discussing humanism because we keep constantly in mind that we are touching necessarily at the same time, as an instrinsic

---

[1] Compare the later explicitation in *Unterwegs zur Sprache,* p. 196: „Denn der Mensch ist nur Mensch, insofern er dem Zuspruch der Sprache zugesagt, für die Sprache, sie zu sprechen, gebraucht ist". Furthermore, upon reading „Das Ereignis ist das Unscheinbarste des Unscheinbaren, das Einfachste des Einfachen, das Nächste des Nahen und das Fernste des Fernen, darin wir Sterblichen uns zeitlebens aufhalten" (p. 259) — and, of course, „aufhalten" is the ethos-dwelling of man —, we recognize immediately the same thought concerning Being in the famous passage of the Letter on pages 19-20.

correlate, the question always in the background of his thought: Being. What we do, then, is to indicate, rather than explicate the presence of the Being-question. Such a process is often more fruitful than bravely trying to point directly at "Being". As far as concerns the ultimate value of Heidegger's thought, we are in fact asking the question in its most concise, concentrated and chalanging form. When asking what place man has in history, we are asking whether he is a spectre, a spectator or a creator; correlatively implied is whether Being is the only reality, the over-riding One, whether Being is History or merely has a history, or, finally whether Being is such that man is also a creator with some type of participation involved. But what would such a series of implied questions have to do with ethics? One's conception of Being and its rôle determines the weight and importance of man's own being and hence the scope of action that is opened to him.

According to the rôle defined or granted by Being, man will be able to stand before the manifestative power of art, language, the word, the sacred and, perhaps, eventually God — all dimensions of Heidegger's elaboration which must enter into the question of humanism and imply "ethical" action. But to spell out this action in any detail may not be necessary, if as Heidegger does, one thinks through the reality of "humanitas", for then the explicitation of the ethical, not as some extrinsic action or law, is the "natural" (*wesentlich*) resultant. Why? Because if one describes humanism in terms of man's relation to Being and its history — to truth and language —, then has not one essentially oriented the question of the ethical quest for authentic action? For Heidegger this would seem sufficient in view of the history of Western thought whose elaboration of the ethical degenerates into law, rules and regulations detached from the original élan of man's ethos such that they inhibit rather than foster authentic action and being-in-the-world. Certainly this last point will be brought out in the Letter but more important is the insistence that the ethical arises "naturally" (with all the verbal force of *wesen* and *anwesen*): a coming into presence, prior to any distinction between theory and practice.

But what rôle does man really have? It would be very difficult, if not impossible, to ascertain because we eventually come up against a central ambiguity in Heidegger's whole thought — and it lies pivotally here in the Letter from the very first page on: the use of the genitive case. In many a crucial passage it cannot be judged as either subjective or objective, nor even primarily as one or the other, this is so particularly in the use of the word "being" as in "des Seins". Put simply, as applied to language, the ambiguity can be read as "man's speaking of Being", "Being's speaking in man", "man speaking Being's word", "Being's word is man's authentic speaking", etc. Such is the situation that at times we seem to have a truly human, responsible activity and grounds for a non-illusionary humanism; at other times, we find a man who, if faithful to Heidegger's *Denkweg*, will, like a sheep, move out of Plato's Cave, led out by "Being's" presence. The metaphor of man as the Shepherd of Being (or Being's shepherd of beings) is indeed ambiguous. Is man merely a watcher or one who looks out with active responsibility?

This ambiguity persists in the Letter though it moves somewhat in favor of Being, a movement confirmed by "later" Heidegger who is able to say that language is Being's thing, much, perhaps, as the contemporary American idiom would say that "Being is doing its thing". Nevertheless, we have not necessarily resolved the fundamental ambiguity because we come more fully into a sphere where the categories of objective and subjective do not obtain. This is why Heidegger points poetically to the inseparability of language and Being, and of man's action in the "proximity" of the truth of Being as inseparable from what this Nearness of presence accomplishes.

Certainly, as far as the Letter is concerned, we do have a fundamental ambiguity and rather than try to resolve it, we should ask why Heidegger intends perhaps to maintain it. Ambiguity could speak more than mere words — *if* we meet it as that which invites us to think ("das, was zu denken gibt"), if we meet it "poetically" as a sign. It would then be an attempt to situate man in that clime and in that realm where Being pervades such that what Being says, is precisely Being's "thing"

("Sache"), and what man says authentically is thereby a "coming to the word". In the ultimate sense, it may well be nonsense to ask the question in such a way as to imply what man alone could say or do, as some being unto his very own; for, surely, he cannot so ek-sist authentically. Yet, if we are at times inclined to so interpret the movement of Heidegger's intention, there are so many passages, even just within the Letter, as well as his very mode of proceeding, that we can make out a good case that man has not the ability to enter into a "meeting" that transforms presence into real, historical signification, and that man has nothing at all to say and must simply await for the truth, the light and the Logos, guaranteed by the eventual coming-into-presence of Being's presence as "proximity". Surely we cannot admit that man would have no more say than a puppet on Being's stage.

It is clear that our concern is not overly narrow though it will deal mainly with Heidegger's own ideas on the subject of humanism and ethics, and the consequent influence upon so many thinkers who have either analyzed, or simply imbibed, his thought. The reader, however, will find a secondary interest that is not limited to the question of Heideggerian thought. Its first aspect is an *hermeneutical* problem: the text has not only an horizontal divergence of interpretations, many of which are incompatible, but also a vertical one where most are not necessarily incompatible, since the question becomes to what extent a symbolic reading is intended by the author and to what extent it is readable. The second aspect, again of greater interest perhaps than Heideggerian analysis as such, is the tension between an author's idea and the philosophical, chosen method together with its original intention. By this we mean that Heidegger's handling of the question of humanism has greater interest than just the philosophical idea that it proffers. For here we find a fundamental tension that all serious philosophical thinking encounters: how to preserve some valid insight in relationship to a greater, or more fundamental question? In our author's case: how preserve and somehow develop what could be called a "human vocation" in the context of an "ontology" where Being is the principal question, where Being does not only have the final say but, apparently, also the first say ?

We have just mentioned the hermeneutical. Under this heading, we would like to relate some general, but key introductory, material: the reason for our critical bibliography, the "unsaid" in Heidegger, his demarcation of thought and the neutrality of his language and, finally, the overcoming process. We shall then be positioned to turn to an immediate introduction of our work.

We have selected our bibliography from some 1100 books and articles on the basis of their pertinence to humanism and ethics. The wide divergence of interpretation which we have summarized arose through an inductive approach to the data. It was not controlled by some a priori, though the data did confirm to an amazing degree our own prior analysis of the text of the Letter as being most ambiguous, at least on one level of interpretation; consequently, we became more convinced of the need of an interpretation on another level characterized by some conformity with Heidegger's own hermeneutical approach. The fantastic profusion of interpretations proved not only the need of "de-mythologizing" most of the Heideggerian literature but also one of eventually greater importance: the need to apply some of Heidegger's valid hermeneutic tools to his own thought and thus to discover more clearly the nature of those tools as they themselves are at work. Commentators do not first attempt to "let be" the text, to discover *what* invites the reader to think — a "what" that is essentially symbolic and poetic. In letting the text speak, one must at the same time read with it the unspoken and the unsaid. It is a remarkably striking fact that most of the very people who have been influenced by Heideggerian hermeneutics turn to his work as if it were something out-there, rather than as a text that lives originally according to the very hermeneutics which they are anxious to employ elsewhere.

In our exposition of the text, we have, by and large, chosen the most difficult passages to read. But why ? Though there are many other passages which are, at least at first sight, unambiguous, they become ambivalent when considered in the context of the movement of Heidegger's thought, because they eventually rest upon the difficult passages. The majority of these are the most incisive and the most pregnant — with the unsaid. They control the reading of the Letter.

It is due to the inherent limitations of conceptualistic language as well as to some of its unwanted historical associations that Heidegger increasingly moves towards the poetic; furthermore, as he comes at once "nearer and further" from the fundamental question(s), there is, as it were, a constant shifting of ground, or better, of attitude as part of the same interpretative behavior, as he comes to grips, perhaps, with the ungraspable. The whole forms one hermeneutic situation, out of whose "deficient" wholeness the "unsaid"[2] is supposed to come forth with positive signification. If, on the other hand, one approaches the text with Cartesian or Carnap exigencies, he will find utter non-sense. Yet, to varying degrees, many a commentator has done so. The question is not whether an intelligent person comes to the text but coming to the text with "intelligence" related to a *Befindlichkeit*.

Nevertheless, at times, one has good reasons to think that Heidegger is merely talking in riddles. But perhaps a more serious shortcoming is a demarcation set to his own thought. As we shall see in the exposition of the text, he maintains that whatever limit there may be to thought is not to be set by man, but by Being. This may be true, but too convenient, because in practice, what matters is man's finding such a limit and recognizing it — which, moreover, becomes in the same act a form of transcendence.

Heidegger places a distinction between the thinker and the poet. True, it is usually one of identity and difference, and one of only different modes of arrival; but as Heidegger moves on, especially towards some apophatic, the poet seems to move in

---

[2] Rather than indicating some of Heidegger's technical remarks on the unsaid, let the following encomium suffice, which he utters at the beginning of *Platons Lehre von der Wahrheit*, to which, significantly enough, the publishing of the Letter was originally appended: "Die 'Lehre' eines Denkers ist das in seinem Sagen Ungesagte, dem der Mensch ausgesetzt wird, auf dass er dafür sich verschwende".

a distinct realm inaccessible to the thinker — we cannot in this introduction examine how the term "thinker" may have been intrinsically altered into a symbolic form, called the "poet". We know, of course, that the term "thinker" has supplanted "philosopher" which in turn is marked off from "theologian". This last demarcation creates problems, if for no other reason than the methodological in view of Heidegger's language.

Heidegger admits to a language that he would not have employed had it not been for theology and his earlier studies. He insists, however, that its terms are without their prior contents and signification. As expected, this leads to great confusion, beginning as early as with Bultmann. Be that as it may, we find a serious, intrinsic difficulty, especially in view of Heidegger's own stress on the nature of historicity. If he can empty out terms or put hermetically sealed brackets around words that grew out of a culture and out of a biblical and theological tradition, he cannot negate on the reader's behalf the content-reference that this language still signifies in the culture through which it is expressed. Furthermore, and more fundamental, how can he succeed *geschichtlich* in doing so? For language is a past-present oriented into the future by the very nature of history. In attempting to regain the pristine purity of language, one must act through an insight existing today. Though going back and enriched by the past, one cannot grasp the past as such, for it is not repeatable as such. Part of the very insight comes from within the culture of today so that one cannot stand outside by a fiat of the will and look at it with a stranger's spectator-eye — and so, too, the past.

It is precisely the neutrality — or better, perhaps, the intended neutrality — of Heidegger's speech that lends it to the malleable hands of anxious theologians. We may not be excessively critical of them if we see the difficulty of knowing to what extent Heidegger could have succeeded in "de-onto-theo-logizing" language. Perhaps he has meant to preserve somehow (rather than assert) their theological, mystical and/or sacred referent while waiting for the time that will allow their utterance in a non "metaphysical" way, the latter term being used exactly in the sense that he criticizes in the Letter. For, after all, he did not have to choose such language in the first place and, secondly, as it is clear in the Letter, he awaits a further explicitation of language, at least on "Being's part". This point would be quite consonant with the development of the original phenomenological procedure found in *Being and Time*. The fact, however, that he insists that he does not have as yet the language to speak about the sacred *should* militate against the wreckless use of Heidegger's speech made by some theologians. For our part, we ultimately have a more fundamental problem; we do not see how Heidegger can *stand* in time to await the explicitation which becomes less and less a task of man's *Interpretation* and more and more an *Aus-legung des Seins* — that is, an interpretative laying-out on Being's part. Or, put differently in order to express our quite personal judgement, Heidegger stands in the world rather than with the world such that there can only come about some untainted arrival of the Event (Ereignis) of the Word (Logos) and of man to Language (Sprache). Clearly, this would present a problem for a "humanism", or whatever word one may choose, that would allow man to have his place in the Sun. We cannot accept any shadow of suspicion that man is simply in the Cave waiting to be let out, come the time. As far as we are concerned, and we hope the reader shall be persuaded, the Letter is the central symbol of all this and the confusion and diversity of interpretations merely confirms the point.

Heidegger has taken on the task of overcoming (Überwindung) metaphysics. Since the nature of this process will come out in some detail in our exposition, we wish merely to point out its link with his hermeneutic approach: this task is concretely identified with his very effort to recuperate the (Being-) meaning of language. "Overcoming" is essentially a positive process: destruction-retrieving. The problem arises from the fact that if one moment fails, then the whole process does. Thus, if the destruction is not at the same time the opening that recaptures what has fallen into "forgetfulness", then the process does not open up the level of positive signification. If it succeeds, what remains to be done is the ever unending explicitation, i.e., *Auslegung,* with all of Heidegger's splendid ambiguities, reserved, ultimately, to poetic comportment. Furthermore, the overcoming is the means whereby Heidegger now puts forward the entire question of Being. If his approach should stop at the negative moment, then (but not according to his intention), the reality of man is at stake for the sake of Being's; if it should succeed positively, the nature of human exitence allowing for real ethical behavior and a true humanism remains an open question.

Having just considered some of the central issues of Heidegger's thought, we are now in a position to introduce our work on his Letter which, we are convinced, lies at the very centre of these issues.

We mentioned at the outset that the Letter brings out "latent interpretations" of prior works; this is especially so with *Being and Time.* Actually, according to one's bias, one will speak of a new interpretation, or of a continuous and coherent one, or even of a twisted one in view of an "apologia pro philosophia sua". We shall, however, centre the broad question of continuity on the notion of humanism and its concomitant idea of a fundamental ethic in order to seek what ground there is *in* the text for such a bias. In this way we shall let the text "be" in order to discover something of the ambivalent ground on which Heidegger stands while pointing towards a "humanism" of a new "dimension", as he puts it. It is no easy task to discover this ground and to summarize Heidegger's idea; furthermore, our own concise readings of the text make it no easier at the outset. Therefore, it seems best to ask, first of all in a general manner, about Heidegger's intention in regard to the place of humanism in his philosophy and about the general types of interpretations without seeking the specific content of such a humanism, since this point is indeed the crux of the question.

The Letter seizes the opportunity to clear up many misunderstandings, while revealing a somewhat apological tone. In the framework of this "corrective" attitude, Heidegger leads us through a progression of his basic philosophical thought to tell us mainly what it is not. We may summarize it through a series of neither-nor's: his thought is neither theism nor atheism, neither a theory nor a praxis, neither logic nor irrationalism, neither metaphysics nor ontology, neither value philosophy nor indifferentism, neither anthropology nor antihumanism, neither psychologism nor existentialism... .Within these neither-nor's is to be inscribed his idea of "humanism". Strange as it may seem at first, each one of these categories which Heidegger has formally rejected is used to identify his notion of humanism. Evidently, the first distinction that one must make is between the author's intention and the de facto success or failure in carrying it out.

Thus, there can be no quarrel with a philosopher who opposes an interpretation contrary to Heidegger's formal declarations provided that he 1) recognizes Heidegger's formal disclaimer, 2) distinguishes Heidegger's intention from what is to be judged as the de facto result of this thought, 3) gives some grounding for his judgement and 4) that his argumentation is, at least according to one aspect, lined up intrinsically with the thought of Heidegger lest we have a mere "lis de verbis" or a categorical whitewashing of a place where Heidegger never stood.

Though this procedure seems all too obvious, unfortunately a respect for such basic criteria of critique is not always found among commentators, especially those of Heidegger. Indeed, they have been some who have merely taken up a fad fed by fanciful fiction. To try to enter into the climate of Heideggerian thinking, it must be admitted, takes more time and effort than have often been expended, perhaps with the justified feeling that it is not, after all, proportionately worthwhile. Be that as it may, we find unqualified commentators on all sides: German speaking thinkers not especially well grounded in contemporary philosophy; non Germanic philosophers insufficiently grounded in the German language. Thus, it is not too surprising that we have in English no translation of the Letter worthy of the name "trans-lation".

Apart from those who bring an unpardonable bias or ignorance there is, most fortunately, a good number of highly qualified men who come to terms in a fruitful and friendly dissonance with the question at hand. We shall see three principal classes of interpretations develop and we shall note that in each there are some who make a very cogent case. Since each class can to some extent be well grounded, they do not necessarily exclude one another.

Heidegger's thought is either de facto, or de jure, or both reducible to an "anti-humanism", a "meta-humanism" or an "authentic humanism". Rarely, of course, will we find an author approaching one of these pure positions, but they will be most useful to get through the mass of data.

This wide range of interpretation does not, however, produce pure dissonance. For there is a certain harmony in the way serious interpretations tend to revolve about some central idea, expressed or understood. An example is the meaning of the Heideggerian expression "Entsprechen"; according to one's way of understanding it either as a simple or structural correspondence leaving no room for a real human rôle, or as a correspondence in view of some ideal or eschatological idea of history, or finally, as a true responding activity, the above threefold division of humanism is had. Though, as we shall see, there are many ways at arriving to one of these classifications; nevertheless, the question of the type of "correspondence" involved is a determinant of the truly central question of this Letter and, indeed, perhaps of Heidegger's entire philosophical effort: the question of "overcoming" metaphysics.

Is one justified in attaching any serious importance to the idea of humanism in Heidegger ? At first glance such a question appears out of place, for «humanism» is indeed the title of the Letter. Yet many would respond negatively to our question. The given title is no adequate answer if one maintains that the subject of humanism is a mere occasion, indeed, the long awaited excuse to launch off on a whole group of pent-up subjects. Without denying that it is *an* occasion, since he is after all answering a letter on this subject, it is no mere excuse. Heidegger is truly interested in wanting to propose the basis for a deeper and more profound "humanism". We can show in our reading of the text that his thinking on humanism is an integral part of a central theme, namely the overcoming of metaphysical thinking. This fact makes the subject of humanism a true correlative of the method, it makes humanism an integral question of his thought.

According to the nature of the overcoming process, one will be able to speak of a species of our threefold division of "anti-", "meta-" and "authentic" humanism. This will become clear as we try to evaluate the prior possibilities of various areas of conflicting interpretations. To anticipate one form of specifying this, it would seem that an intrinsic success of the process would give us one key example of a meta-humanism, its failure would give us one type of anti-humanism. What about those who hold for the "authentic" or for a veritable ground of a new and profound humanism? The success of the Heideggerian approach would not alone justify such an interpretation. Why? "Authenticity" to have real meaning implies a real historical content, a ground for true creative and responsible action. The possibility of authenticity is by no means assured by acclaiming an "overcoming" success. For the interpretation favoring authenticity must be coupled with an affirmative answer to the central idea mentioned above: "Entsprechen". In the last analysis the interpreter of Heidegger who holds for a true, authentic humanism must solve at least these two points: the positive outcome of his overcoming of metaphysics and the positive human content of *Entsprechung* as response and responsability.

What does Heidegger mean by "humanism"? What does he reject? What type of "new" humanism would he favor? We shall bring out these questions as they naturally arise from our reading of the text. As a general orientation, however, we must make a few remarks that are justifiable precisely because they are highly qualified in order to keep fundamental questions open. At the outset is this especially an important value, since there is a certain fundamental and minimal statement to be made that keeps open a maximum of possibilities and thus wards off a tendency to make prior restricting identifications. Of such a need, there is no doubt. Few words are so tendentious as "humanism". Our observations are intended as an introductory bridge to the Heideggerian optic.

"Humanism" should be neither identified with, nor delimited as a substitute for, religious sentiment, attitude or reflection. Nor is it to be identified with a philosophy as such, much less a metaphysic. On the other hand, it is a truly philosophical question and attitude; it can also be a philosophical comportment and, as such, may have religious connotations. In searching to circumscribe the meaning of humanism, one must not delimit it a priori; rather, one must turn to a basic "phenomenological" and/or philosophical questioning: what rôle does man have in being man, what action is man's in becoming man and, hence, what *action* is thus essentially becoming to man ? We note that the Letter begins precisely with the words: "Wir bedenken das Wesen des *Handelns* noch lange nicht entschieden genug" (we underscore).

What is man's "place" in history ? For certainly this seems an unavoidable question of "humanism". Yet at the beginning one must positively refrain from annointing some idea of "man-place", whether it be as a materialistic or spiritual evolutionist idea, or as a humanistic idealism where "humanistic" implies the existence, or even only the possibility, of merely human "values". One should begin with a search for the notion of the *human,* unrestricted by "humanistic" or "humane". One must begin with an effort at considering man's historical rôle with no arbitrary foreclosing of his and/or history's horizons.

In asking the question about the general nature of humanism, one has to come to grips with lived experience as pointing back to a fundamental grounding experience and pointing forward at the same time to its historically oriented dimension. If Heidegger is correct, however, one need not at the outset explicitate personal experience which, as truly lived experience, opens upon the question of history as event, an event that cannot be foreclosed as to its nature: the event of Being, of truth, of the holy, of the gods, of God... as expressed by the sequence of the famous passage of the Letter in which Heidegger sketches out what is possible at least according to his intention and perhaps also according to the actual development of his philosophy within which there is a search to define humanism as the "humanistas of homo humanus". But in the final evaluation of his idea of humanism, or of anyone else's for that matter, one must come to the question: is there room for true human experience in the realization of this idea, or, for example, is the human factor so structuralized as to be squeezed out of its historical frame?

We may say in Heideggerian language that "humanism", precisely by going beyond the word, states that *there is* a human *vocation* that must *ek-sist*. It would be no easy task to determine the historical and existentiel meaning and content of such a "vocation". As a minimal statement, however, Heidegger does affirm "a call of Being": a call of Being to man and a responding call of man to Being such that there is not necessarily, however, more than an explicitation of the idea that somehow there must be a fundamental "correspondence". If, of course, humanism in Heidegger should assert no more than some mathematical type of correspondence, then human "answering" would indeed be a destitute "poverty" of Being. Yet Heidegger seems to be saying much more. But how much more? And may he let himself say it in his chosen framework? These questions will help to underline the fantastic spread of opinions on this subject.

Thus, we are not going to try to resolve, let alone solve the ambiguities of Heidegger's thought. On the contrary, we intend to *re-establish* the central ambiguities in relation to humanism and ethics. It is on this basis that the great spread of the critical bibliography will be laid out. We hope to clear some ground in seeing a diverging opinion rather than a simple opposition of opinions.

It is now clear that our interest in the possibilities of Heidegger's "humanism" is not, at least in this present work, directed to our own personal evaluation of them, and much less to our "redoing" somehow such a humanism. Though such is our purpose, it is quite obvious that our critique will betray some of our personal views — we need make no apology for not being in a pure presuppositionless state. On the other hand, there will come about a certain convergence suggested at a deeper level of analysis which, without elaborating it as such, will give us, nevertheless, the opportunity of formulating some questions on "humanism" that need much more consideration than they have heretofore received. For example, the relationship of Heidegger's notion of "de-divinization" to a possible "de-humanization" and, at another level, that of the "death of God" to a "death of man".

As we have stated, the attempt to consider a "humanism" within a greater framework of thought and in accordance with an adopted method constitutes a problematic that is not merely "Heideggerian". By pointing out the tension, by criticizing simplistic interpretations, by indicating the levels of non-contradictory interpretations, by re-establishing an ambiguity at the heart of the matter — that ambiguity without which no philosophy can be fruitful — we hope to take part in the philosophic enterprise and we hope especially, since this is our immediate purpose, to provide a tool which invites others to this enterprise.

In the following part, we shall make a selective reading of the Letter in order to summarize Heidegger's notion of "humanism" and "ethics" and, at the same time, to bring out the main areas out of which will arise the conflicting interpretations. Handling both of these aims together will assure us a better chance to present his view without imposing our own. Part III will consist of an *enchaînement* of the principal interpretations drawn from our bibliography and ordered according to the main classifications developed in Part II. Finally, one will find the selected critical bibliography representing the entire gamut of interpretations.

II

A READING OF THE LETTER

We believe that a selective reading of the Letter, following as closely as possible its orginal order, is the most valid way to discover the elements to be used in trying to sketch Heidegger's notion of humanism and to uncover, as they occur, the various areas of ambiguity which give rise to a legitimate divergence of interpretations. In so doing, we shall clarify the three principal classifications already mentioned and we shall see that the multiple reasons that induce one to think along these lines also overlap one another. All references to the Letter (HB: "Über den Humanismus") are made according to its separate printing*; *all* italics are ours. We place as distinct headings the key pagination of each reading in order to facilitate later reference in studying the critical bibliography and in order to guide the reader's eye through the present development.

[HB, 5]

A selective linking of the first page of the Letter will set up the framework in which the question of humanism arises. By the very approach herein implied, the question will be inescapable but by no means can we hasten to read into this framework a real historical content. The Letter begins thus:

> Wir bedenken das Wesen des *Handelns*. ...das *Wesen* des Handelns ist das *Vollbrigen*. ... Das *Denken* vollbringt den

---

* KLOSTERMANN, Frankfurt A.M., 1947. At the end of our study, the reader will find a correlated pagination to the other standard text: *Platons Lehre von der Wahrheit. Mit einem Brief über den "Humanismus"*. Francke Verlag Bern, 1947. Zweite Auflage, 1954. For this work, we use the symbol: PW.

> *Bezug* des Seins zum Wesen des Menschen. ...Das Denken handelt, indem es denkt. ... Das Denken dagegen lässt sich vom Sein in den *Anspruch* nehmen, um die Wahrheit des Seins *zu sagen*. ... Denken ist *l'engagement* par l'Etre pour l'Etre.

Let us first rapidly paraphrase: in considering action we should come down to its essence: a "fulfilment", a bringing forth of that which already is, i.e., which is in relation to Being. Action brings out *this* relation as it concerns the essence of man. Which action does this? Thinking. Thought is acting is so far as it thinks. How does such thinking take place? Thinking lets itself be taken up by Being in the demanding word that Being addresses to man. For what purpose? To speak the truth of Being. Then what is the core reality of such thinking? It is "l'engagement par l'Etre pour l'Etre".

Thus the essence of action is a thinking framed and nurtured by Being. Since this point is so fundamental to the very nature of man, the question will naturally arise: do we have here the ground for a (new) humanism? Are we not talking of a fulfilment that somehow belongs at one and the same time to man and to Being? For such "thinking" must touch man; it must explain and indeed historicize the very make-up of man. But we cannot rush headlong into this line of thinking because a closer look at this passage reveals that what is clear is nothing more than the relative relationships: essence, man, Being, thought, action. We do not know immediately what real content these have nor what reference they have to historical man.

What is certain is that the question of humanism is going to be intimately bound with a being which, by virtue of its historicity, is to speak the truth, understood as a disclosing of the relationship of Being to history. One would like to speak here of a human *task*. But the full connotations of this expression should not be read into the text. The ideas of "Anspruch" and "vollbringen" allow only the statement of a *relationship* according to which "man" "is ordered" for speaking a disclosing relation. Since the nature of this relationship is unclear, we cannot readily infer what human reality, if any, is being talked about. It is because of this ambiguity that the widest interpretation is possible. To set off its limits, let us state the two pure limit-cases that have evolved: some will see implied here a fundamental human task and a way to authentic living, proclaiming Heidegger a prophet of a full-blown humanism; others will see a closed, abstract relation incapable not only of asking the question about humanism but also radically closed to any consideration of the very possibility of even asking, except through some word game, what man is.

In short, the starting point within the framework suggested by the first page of the Letter reveals a tension between its formalized expression and its possible content. This leads either to a consideration of a human rôle in historical reality or to a contemplation of man's "place" within a structured thought and/or a structural frame of Being. On the other hand, the tension between these two poles can be so read as to favor a resolution into one of the three main classes of "humanism": anti-, meta-, or authentic "humanism" — according to the way one interprets the fundamental relation as being essentially non-relevant, transcendentally significant, or coinciding existentially with "entsprechen".

One can refrain more easily, at the very beginning, from imposing foreign categories on Heidegger's "humanism" when one considers that the word "Vollbringen" gathers up the full sweep of a nebulous start. For example, in what sense are the following questions *distinct or identified in fact* with one another: fulfilment of man, or of man's history, or of his pure historicity? Or of man's Being, as Being-there, or merely of man's There as There-being? And/or fulfilment of Being, of Being's call, of Being's thinking, of Being's History? Is there a place for fulfilment of self? Wherein lies the "essence of humanism"? Is a philosophical humanism possible or impossible? If possible, is it open or closed?

[HB, 5/6]

Before bringing together the material, we shall deliberately point out one passage then another that seem to favor different interpretations since we must beware of being over-systematic, if we wish to respect the author's thought.

"Die Geschichte des Seins trägt und bestimmt jede condition et situation humaine" — "The history of Being sustains and determines every human condition and situation". Such a statement with its context can foster the "structuralist" interpretation of Heidegger's humanism; namely, "man" is but a mouthpiece mouthing the language which is given to him by "History" and through whom Being speaks. Man erroneously prides himself as doing something which would truly touch and realize the being that he is. On the other hand, this "history" can be taken as a determinant weighing upon man's present outlook according to the way he has understood this essential question of philosophy: "how does he stand with Being?". In this case, such "history" is really the history of man's interpretation of Being, his past efforts at asking the question of the sense of Being, an asking which is actual and already a future determinant. In the first case we have History (of Being) to which man is subordinate and/or coordinated; in the second case, we have man's historicity linked in creating the very essence of history, the interpretation of how he stands with Being. Out of this, a middle position comes forth: man's historicity in its very authenticity is defined in terms of manifesting the History of Being. But this statement is reversible: History takes up the historicity of man. This assertion in turn leads some commentators to return to the structuralist interpretation: History is in so far as it takes up the historicity of man into the realm of Being, where Being holds sway. Thus, man's historicity and his action, his doing, his speaking, his situation are, in so far as they really exist, identified with the History of Being. It would be difficult not to conceive of this as a Structure. If indeed some "return" to a structuralist interpretation through a further analysis of the third or middle view, others had never abandoned it. For these see, even in the existentially nuanced second position only the bones of scaffolded thought: when Heidegger speaks of man's effort, task, or realization, they read the word "man" as simply a "place" where this "takes place".

In any case, the notion of history, understood as man being the There of Being and the place of Its revelation, more than any other factor ultimately determines, in the most fundamental sense of Heideggerian phenomenology, the very possibility of what it means for man to have a "vocation", to have a say in being what he is to be. The nature and the possibility of a "humanism" is thereby fixed. Furthermore, we must also retain the following which will come out as we progress through the Letter: "thinking", "doing" and "speaking" form such a strict relationship that the critique of one will not leave the other intact. These three are factors of "humanism".

[HB, 7]

"Das Denken ist — dies sagt: das Sein hat sich je geschicklich seines Wesens angenommen": "Being has always in the manner of destiny [by imparting itself] taken charge of its essence". This definition of foundational thinking is given in the very paragraph where the author takes up the question, "Comment redonner un sens au mot 'Humanisme'?", which will be developed later (p. 31). This question has a double nuance: how to give back or retrieve the sense of a word and how to give anew a meaningful sense. In typical fashion, he puts off the question of the word humanism and indicates that he will give it a meaning through a unique, "doubled" process: the giving of a new meaning by retrieving the old. This he links up immediately with the fundamental point: man is man precisely in that he "thinks". This thinking appears less as a task for man than as a "mission" im-parted by Being, a mission that Being works out *in* man's essential thinking. This of course recalls the famous play on words between such "im-parting" or "destination" and "history" (geschicklich und geschichtlich).

In the manner in which one asserts that Heidegger maintains the transcendence of Being and cares likewise to read him in Hegelian or Fichtean terms, can one easily conceive of Heidegger's thought as a "meta-humanism". In so far, however, as one insists on Heidegger's self-avowed differences from such a tradition as, for example in his stressing the finitude of man, the openness of *Geschichtlichkeit* within the finitude of the *Geschickliche,* does many a commentator reduce his thought to an anti-humanism either because it is felt that the result is a structuralist type of thought, or, — which does not necessarily exclude holding the first reason —, because Heidegger has failed in the positive task of overcoming metaphysics. The link-up of this reasoning will appear later. Let us for the moment stress only the first point: "geschicklich seines Wesens angenommen": in so far as it favors a mission rather than a human task and emphasizes correlatively Being's imparting itself *geschichtlich* to man as the very essenc-ing of history, a type of structuralist interpretation is easily favored. For then man seems present only *to* Being speaking in history, indeed, to Being speaking history. Now, since speaking, thinking and doing form one essential process, it is Being that speaks, thinks and does History within which, as a framework, man stands... stands, presumably at "attention".

[HB, 7/8]

Such an interpretation of the text must, however, be balanced with what immediately follows: *Annehmen* is linked to *Mögen* taken in the multiple sense of desire, power, possibility and love, out of which comes the notion that there is a "gift" of this essence (das Wesen schenken). For Being is the "Vermögend-Mögende". This power-love-possibility allows something to really be (eigentlich zu sein) and, presumably, man to be really what he is in reference to Being. Such a conception would have to mitigate any structuralist interpretation of Heidegger, certainly that type which reduces his thought to anti-humanistic consequences. And, yet, if it does so, it is by no means clear how it may do it in conformity with the rest of Heidegger's view. For "Das Sein als Vermögend-Mögend" seems to point to some concrete historical resolution in man without, however, taking up the prior question of how man may have a positive rôle in this. Thus, this more "humanistic" endeavor in terms of "Gift", love, desire and power may well point instead to some type of resolution beyond the actual historicity of man. It would then favor a "meta-humanism" correlative to Being's "mögend über das Denken und so über das Wesen des Menschen".

In any case, Heidegger closes this consideration with a frightfully ambiguous statement. To the question what is "etwas vermögen" [which we saw, p. 7, was "etwas eigentlich zu sein vermag", and presumably man in his "work"], he answers: "es in seinem Wesen wahren, in seinem Element einbehalten" — "to preserve (guard) it in its essence, to maintain it in its element". This is predicated primarily of Being. Although "wahren" will be taken later as man's mission, sc. "shepherd of Being", there is as yet no hint of some positive rôle for man in this process, unless it be by recalling that "wahren" is to be the "task" of guarding the house of Language, Being's house. In this would somehow reside man's right to be. In terms of thought, language and "action", the essential happening stands in relation to Being as *Mögen*. But such a relation is still suspect as some "correspondence"; if so, the "engagement" (of p. 5) would eventually be a mere product of neo-structuralism. On the other hand, prior to the above, ambiguous, closing statement, the development did not seem to warrant such an interpretation. "...seines Wesens angenommen. Sich einer 'Sache' oder einer 'Person' in ihrem Wesen annehmen, das heisst: sie lieben: sie mögen". Quite evidently this can suggest an historical process in which man has the rôle of a true response. Therefore, it is imperative that we do not categorize Heidegger's thought from a mere sampling of his writing, here or elsewhere.

[HB, 9]

After recalling his own historical interpretation of the de-volution of thought into *téchnê*, i.e., its reduction to a mere instrument (p. 8), Heidegger insists that we have missed the point concerning the nature of language: it is the "house of the truth of Being". Instead, we have considered it an instrument for dominating, for lording it over beings: "... ein Instrument der Herrschaft über das Seiende".

This thought will fit in with the development of the idea that man is not the master of beings but their shepherd. This statement, however, invites the suspicion that since language is not a mere instrument of man, there is "something" substituted for this function. Does the dimension that Heidegger opens up overcome, within the finitude of Dasein, the suspicion that man in his very essence (wesentlich denken und sagen) now stands in relationship to Being as we had, supposedly, falsely conceived the relationship between language and man? In other words, has man become the mere instrument of Being? Or, as previously suggested, the mouthpiece of Being? If so, we now have a form of anti-humanism with no nuance of a meta-humanism. This would be especially so if we consider that this is equivalently saying that man is an instrument of "Language" — with Heidegger's mysterious capitalization of *Lógos*. In this case it is difficult not to think of a new brand of old-fashioned positivism.

This line of reasoning would support those commentators who criticize Heidegger as denying man a real being (Seiende). The logic of this position would require that his thought represent nothing more than pure constructed relationships; for, if man cannot be a being, and if, as it is certain with Heidegger, Being is no being, then whatever "reality" there is historically can be none other than some pure co-relation of one to another, where each is no "being" other than the pure referent to the other and by the other, and vice versa. — This seems even more abstruse than the most refined of trinitarian speculations.

[HB, 10]

This seeming un-doing of man's being would go hand in hand with a neutral type of expression generally found throughout Heidegger terminology:

> "Der Mensch muss, bevor er spricht, erst vom Sein sich wieder ansprechen lassen auf die Gefahr, dass er unter diesem An-

spruch wenig oder selten etwas zu sagen hat. Nur so wird dem Wort die Kostbarkeit seines Wesens, dem Menschen aber die Behausung für das Wohnen in der Wahrheit des Seins wiedergeschenkt".

...it is only in this way that the pricelessness of its essence is restored to the word [and] "to man the lodging for the dwelling in the truth of Being". This too literal a translation indicated by quotation marks puts across an urgent point. Why not say that there is then restored "to man the dwelling where he can live in the truth of Being"? This is indeed the way it is rendered by the English translation. This is undoubtedly better English but it gives a definite personalist connotation, or at least an existentiel one. We must note that the text does not keep the same subject as the passage's beginning. It does not say "... wo *er* in der Wahrheit des Seins wohnt" (or, "wohnen kann/muss" or even "wo er sich ... wohnen lässt"). True, this is but a subtle point but examples abound. This leads one to think that there really is a depersonalized expression according to an original method of bracketing being.

We find through slow and steady accumulation of inaccurate, or at least nuanced translations, a washing away of Heidegger's "neutral" language and thus also of the ambiguity of his thought. Such a process, in which even the translator often becomes mesmerized and no longer thinks "out of" (*aus*) Heidegger, has, we believe, done much to foster the existentiel interpretation opening upon an "authentic" humanism[3].

It is at this juncture of the text that Heidegger returns to

---

[3] Without going into the question that a readable translation often requires, among other things, grammatical transpositions, let us cite as an example, HB, 13: "Noch wartet das Sein dass Es selbst dem Menschen denkwürdig werde". R. Munier's translation, probably the best, gives: "L'Être attend toujours que l'homme se le remémore comme digne d'être pensé". Still, the text would demand in view of Heidegger's "subordination" of man's action: "L'Être attend toujours qu'*Il* devienne rememoré...". At the opposite pole of quality translation, the reader will find at the end of this section some examples of the English rendition which blatantly interject an existentiel reading through the personalization of the text.

the "Anspruch des Seins", since it makes possible "man's taking up" his lodging "für das Wohnen...". It is here that he gives his first "definition" of humanism.

"Humanism" is: "Sinnen und Sorgen, dass der Mensch menschlich sei...", "to reflect and to care that man[homo] be human[humanus] and not unhuman, 'inhuman', i.e., [be] outside his essence". "The humanity of man consists in his essence". There had been the question (on p. 5) of what preparation is had for man to stand in relation to the demanding word of Being. The answer had rested on the nature of thought. This is now seen as "sinnen und sorgen": foundational thinking which is *geschichtlich*, "essential" being defined as also *geschicklich*. This thought is now explicitated and "located" in man's essential humanity which must preserve, by being within this scope, these characteristics of historicity and "destiny" in relation to Being. This will define "humanism" or, at least, its ground.

But this ground has supposedly been lost through the history of humanism. Before seeing in what way he may perhaps preserve this term, Heidegger points out his preference for "Humanitas" over against "Humanismus" which is at best a metaphysically contaminated and blinding term, and takes the occasion to review its "history" and to identify his restatement of humanism as essentially the same task as the overcoming of metaphysics. This will bring us through the ancients up to Nietzsche (pp. 10-15).

Let us examine briefly some aspects of Heidegger's historical critique (pp. 10-12) which allow us to see something of how he situates his own view of humanism, or better his idea of "Humanitas des homo humanus".

"Humanism", understood as the concept, is a Roman phenomenon marking an encounter with Hellinism. The Rennaissance is a repetition of the same over against "Gothic scholasticism". Hence, humanism, histori*cally* understood, always carries with it a "studium humanitatis" going back to Roman antiquity and reviving the Greek notion of *paidéia* as understood by the Romans. To this tradition belong such men as Goethe and Schiller. But not Hölderlin — and so, implicitly, Heidegger places himself apart. Why ? Because humanism is to be grasped not "historisch" but "geschichtlich" and, consequently, "wesentlich".

When one comes to the consideration of humanism as man's effort "to become free for his humanity and to find therein his dignity", then one's ideas about "liberty" and human "nature" are going to determine a specific humanism. Each one of these humanisms, be it Marxist, Sartrian or Christian fails; for, they conceive the very question of humanity in terms of history interpreted metaphysically. We know, of course, that Heidegger has in mind a notion of historicity whose essence is freedom, which in turn is truth (e.g., cf. *Wom Wesen der Wahrheit*).

Heidegger insists that the supposition of a philosophy of being, one neglecting the question of the truth of Being, has been the framework of every attempt to determine the essence of man; each has been "metaphysical" and "humanistic", since every humanism has ignored "the relation of Being *to* the essence of man". Therefore, since "humanism" has been effectively identified with "metaphysics", the destruction of the latter is necessary to recapture the true sense of the question of Being as well as that of *Humanitas*. When we recall that the essential sense of *Humanitas* lies in its essence which is the "thought of Being", then getting back to the original ground of humanism is also the coming to a common ground in view of the overcoming of metaphysics. Thus, Heidegger is prepared to have a double "destruction" at one stroke: that of humanism and that of metaphysics.

This doubled task that Heidegger links up must ultimately be the object of any serious critique of his "humanism". Let us explicitate. Just as it appears from the text that Heidegger is against the *-ism* of "humanism" in view of some deeper meaning of "humanitas of homo humanus", so is he also against metaphysics — always understood as "metaphysics" — in order to reach its true ground. These are the negative moments of the *Überwindung*-process. This fact poses initially two questions: is Heidegger's "anti-humanism" (of which he has been so often accused) just a moment of his philosophical method ?

Put this way, one should answer "yes" — and hurry to qualify it. Yes, at least in so far as it is according to his original intention that it be nothing more than a moment. Is it more? That depends on whether one holds that he has in fact succeeded in overcoming metaphysics to the extent that he has come out of the negative and that he is at least on the path to something, on the *way* to discovering a "sense".

And, yet, even if this is so, the "yes" is open to further qualification. Supposing that the entire process does come off, has something been sacrificed? With the overcoming of metaphysics in its positive import and its consequent reaffirmation of the "primacy of Being", is there left any room for a true historic and historial humanity? For a new "humanism" to *express itself*? Or rather, has the process fragmented, leaving to one side a "negated man" (or at least a severely "diminished" man) along with an affirmation of the Truth, of the Word, of the Holy and of Being...?

From the discourse on the relation of metaphysics and its concept of man (12/13) we can, while making a preliminary clarification of his intention and method in attacking the question of humanism, discover a latent aporia.

[HB, 12]

"Die Metaphysik stellt zwar..." — Metaphysics by positing beings thinks the Being of beings. The trouble is that it does not think the ontological difference, the relation itself of Being, but remains trapped with the forms of beings. It does not seek after the truth of Being. Since this difference is the basis for recognizing authentic philosophy, it is also what is going to define eventually a humanism of a new dimension: not only should man stand in the truth (which is clear from the outset of the Letter) but he should stand therein, such that the "Difference" is revealed. This type of "letting-be" the resultant difference would be the fulfilness of man's essential rôle. It would then be the essence of humanism in its very authenticity. Therefore, since metaphysics does not seek after the truth of Being, it never asks about the manner in which man's essence belongs to the truth of Being ("in welcher Weise das Wesen... gehört"). Being still waits for man.

What is the import of this reasoning? We find ourselves already within the Heideggerian *Kehre* as it touches the essence of man and seeks to redefine, reorient, or perhaps to simply re-think it in terms of Being. Here can be found Heidegger's positive task: to lay the groundwork pointing to a positive and fundamental humanism with a concomitant fundamental ethic. This is, indeed, his *intention,* a new humanism in function of the other "dimension".

We can already sense the aporia that will come out of the Letter. If one intends to lay a groundwork for a humanism, what or how is this going to be worked out even in its most minimal meaningful content? This new humanism will have to be spelled out by experience, *human* experience with a positive creative rôle, unless we hold for some *Geist* playing a game with man.

Is such experience intrinsically conformable to Heidegger's thought? In short the question is this: we either have a structure to be explicitated as ideas, thus moving towards a system — and this could scarcely be Heidegger's intent, — or we have a basic groundwork to be filled, or better to be tilled by human experience. But in the latter case, this requires lived experience, an existenti*el* interpretation which would suggest a type of *Lebensphilosophie.* This kind of approach Heidegger formally denies. Nevertheless, because of this aporia, whether formally recognized or not, many a commentator will insist on the need of understanding Heidegger's approach as existentially involving "authentic" action, experience and humanism. In a word, such an interpretation of Heidegger brackets many of his own disavowals and reads into his "neutral" expression an existentiel content. This approach perfectly complements the other that judges the result of his philosophy by bracketing his intention and finds it anti-humanistic, indeed, anti-human.

[HB, 13]

One cannot readily ascribe an anti-humanism to Heidegger's intention and method. In a short "classic" summary of the radical shortcomings of essentialistic metaphysics, "subject", "person", "spirit" are seen as still bound to a conception of man as a specific difference in relation to animal. Rather, he insists, one must think the essential origin of histo*rial* humanity and to what or where it points. Metaphysics is simply closed to *the* point: "dass der Mensch nur in seinem *Wesen west,* in dem er vom Sein angesprochen wird". What is this statement supposed to indicate? The critique of metaphysics was introduced rhetorically by asking if we were on the right track ("auf dem rechten *Wege*"). The answer is a resounding No. The intention seems equally clear: to find a way. The method is implicit: to put forth an "anti-humanism" in so far as the essence of humanism must go beyond "metaphysics". This approach is then "humanistic" in the sense that it is ordered to finding the way: the way to Being in order to find the way to a true "humanism", the way to language in order to find the way to what it means, *seinsgeschichtlich,* to be man according to the "Humanitas des homo humanus".

Thus the charge of anti-humanism must be based on Heidegger's failure (if such be the case) of overcoming metaphysics.

If his method is looked at or criticized from the viewpoint of history as a discipline, Heidegger's thought is not by this fact alone really attained. It is true, for example, that one can say it is "prehumanist" rather than betraying an anti-humanism because he goes to historic sources prior to the advent of humanism. But, on the other hand, this same thought remains either an anti-humanism or not. To qualify it as "pre-humanist" adds merely the time element in an *historisch* fashion. The question is, and it has always been so for Heidegger, essentially *geschichtlich.*

There is, moreover, another charge that would not depend on the outcome of the overcoming-process. Supposing its success, we may still be faced with a meta-humanism of a vacuous man if the method succeeds only *qua* method, sc., we would then be in a structuralist framework again. This possibility is already present in the passage: "angesprochen". For this requires the addressing of a word which in turn requires the existence of language. In such language lies the ambiguity.

The "new humanism" is to be based on the demanding word addressed to man by Being. This presents three difficulties which is one way or another come through many of the critical attacks on Heidegger.

1) The *Anspruch* is a function of epochal history. For the addresing word is epochal according to Heidegger's own theory of history — already implied on this same page (13): "jedes Vernehmen... gelichtet ist und in seiner Wahrheit sich ereignet". This opens him to the charge of how he can know, or justify, that he is in a position to see more clearly *now* the historical mittance of the word. 2) The *Anspruch* is *the* word of Being. Being is *Lógos*, Being is somehow with a pregiven language which man must come around to "have" — "Nur aus diesem Anspruch 'hat' er 'Sprache'". Such a philosophical position would obviously have its difficulties, including some well discussed by structuralism. 3) Since Being is *Lógos*, man is at once "on the way to" both language and Being. This leads easily into the metahuman interpretation, one form of which is the eschatological framework positing humanism (or more exactly "Humanitas") and language back into history as some ideal. In other words, we would have found a back entrance to Plato's cave through the supposedly real orientation of Heidegger's anti-Platonic diatribe.

In any case, the point of this passage is that, whatever be one's interpretation on the nature of humanism and of man's historic rôle, the "Anspruch" brings about, as its correlative, the definition of man as he is supposed to be, sc., as ecstatic existence dwelling in the word of Being and preserving its manifestative language: "Das Stehen in der Lichtung des Seins nenne ich die Ek-sistenz des Menschen".

[HB, 16]

Through a discourse on the essential "nature" of language Heidegger announces his breakthrough on man's relation to Being and, hence, his basis for a new humanism even though we cannot determine for sure its relationship to historical man.

Animals are situated in a mere environment (*Umgebung*), whereas man's "Umwelt" is a true "world". The difference is not merely that the one is deprived of language but that the other can stand in the "lighting-up of Being". The fundamental "fact" of language is "the clearing-concealing advent of Being itself". This *is* the "Lichtung des Seins". This is also the outcome of the "in-der-Welt-Sein" of *Sein und Zeit*. "Man" will now be described, if not already defined as, "der ekstatische Bezug zur Lichtung des Seins" (p. 17) and, hence, as the *Dasein* (p. 16). This "world" is now the same as the "Offenheit des Seins" (p. 35). Man is the "being" that stands *in* and *at* this juncture: the open-ness of Being, the event of the clearing-concealing language, the advent of Being... in a word, the *Ereignis*. Therefore, man's essence, that which will define his true humanity (and thus be the basis of humanism) is man-in-view-of-the-*Ereignis*. This is why man must then be literally ek-sisting in order to be authentic and, correlatively, — as we have shown elsewhere [4] — why the primacy of Being is had, historically, as language and as revealing and as the process itself.

What this process really is, is difficult to say. For we have come a long way since *Sein und Zeit* — *no matter how* one may interpret the "later Heidegger" in terms of this work. As a minimum for our purpose, what has come about is an explicitation of the "Kehre"; what has come out is the relation which is man or is man's. Dasein is now less referred to Being than to the *event* of language and/or of Being. This "and/or" appears incapable or resolution — within Heidegger.

What is striking about this event is that we now suspect that man is himself the object of a pure gift of language, of the

---

[4] *De l'historicité à l'action: L'herméneutique du comportement.* Ed. Nauwelaerts, 1972, p. 364.

coming of language "and" of the coming of Being... *geschiCKlich*. Indeed, man may be himself the gift in so far as he eksists. We thus wonder what creative power he can have in his own right, as his own potentialities to create language, to create art and culture ... to do whatever falls under the whole gamut of the possibility of a humanism — any humanism. This will obviously be the line of argumentation behind many a critique.

At this point especially we would naturally like to examine the text more closely to see in what sense we are speaking of man, in what sense there is the possibility for human action, in what sense there is an appeal to experience to fill in and work out the relationship between this "new" man in the world of Being — or, at least, "destined" for such a world. And, yet, it is precisely here that such a line of questioning would be stopped cold. Heidegger interjects a statement that should make all cautious before undertaking an existenti*el* interpretation (which fact has not discouraged too many): "Der Satz: 'Der Mensch ek-sistiert' antwortet nicht auf die Frage, ob der Mensch wirklich sei oder nicht but answers the question on the 'essence' of man" — which brings us back to the difficulties at the beginning of the text.

This proposition so obviously exacts a type of structuralist interpretation that it is suspect. If Heidegger had affirmed "wirklich ist", the implied question would have been a "who" or a "what". This, of course, is anathema to Heidegger. Of such stuff is the objectifying process of metaphysics made up. It misses the "Wesende der seinsgechichtlichen Ek-sistenz", specifically man as *Da-sein* (and "Wurf", "schickend Geschichtlichkeit", "Wesen"). If this is so, an apparently unambiguous statement is rooted deeply in his method rather than in a simple affirmation. Is this not meant to be only an instance of the process of overcoming? Then one must judge once again according to the larger context and the "objective" merit of the method and whether or not it eventually succeeds.

Be that as it may, other difficulties already seen arise from a different angle: does the *Da* of man as *Da-sein* permit us to speak consistently within Heidegger's thought, of man as a real being? This difficulty springs out of the relation of the "Da" *to* History, Language and Being. The second comes forth from the pages before us (15-17): Heidegger does not want man emptied and pre-empted by a secularized theological explanation. But has he done the same to man in reference to "Lógos", "Sprache" and "Ereignis"? This point brings up a subsidiary question which is found implied in very few authors: with his insistence upon an *Ent-götterung* is there not also at the same time a de-humanization? For, if the process of overcoming metaphysics with its concomitant notions of "person", "value", etc. is not successful, we are then left with an *Ent-humanisierung*. In such a case the possibility of humanism and of "humanitas des homo humanus" is "kaput". Therefore, we arrive at another and somewhat more subtle form of argumentation in favor of an anti-humanism.

[HB, 18]

We now come to the reason for Heidegger's writing of this Letter and to his explicit denial of the charge of anti-humanism. We recall that we can not simply deny the intention of the author; the possibility, however, of his thought being radically anti-humanistic — a possibility by no means unreal — is a question of the *de facto* result of his method and of his philosophizing. The levels of critical interpretation are not to be confused.

"Damit wir Heutigen jedoch in die Dimension der Wahrheit des Seins gelangen... erst... wie das Sein den Menschen angeht und wie es ihn in den Anspruch nimmt". — "That we today may get to the dimension of the truth of Being... we must first make clear how Being concerns man and how it lays its claim upon him", that is, how it addresses to him its demanding word. In terms of the subject matter this statement equivalently says why we have need today to speak out for a *Grundhumanismus*.

Why is this particularly so today? If we read Heidegger correctly, it is a question of epochal history. We still have remnants of metaphysical and theo-logical thinking in the new form of technicity — in fact we may be at the high point of such thinking. To get to the question of man is to go back to the question of Being and, hence, to that of being man. But this is impossible except by overcoming together all forms of metaphysical thinking because they constitute fundamentally only one basic destiny of historico-historial thought. To retrieve the original of the past is the same as to ask today how the "Anspruch" comes upon man, it is the same as laying down a way for the future. What is essential in this basic destiny of history is the essential *mittance* of Being to man in which the essence of being man is to be discovered in an historial way. The overcoming process is locked up in the "reversal" or better in the *kehrende Frage* of Time and Being, Being and Time, Man and Being, Being and Man... and only derivatively of Being and Nothing. The question of Being essentially involves that of "Da-Sein" precisely as a "kehrende Frage". In this sense, the Letter is much more than an occasional treatment of humanism in view of taking up the main themes of Heidegger, it stresses the ground for grounding a philosophy of "humanitas" in so far as the question of Being is inseparately that of "Da" and "Sein".

This intimate relationship between man and Being, has always been a preoccupation with Heidegger. The emphasis, or at least the manner of his questioning, has moved from the sense of Being to the truth of Being and finally to the language of Being as a gradual explicitation within, or through, the *Kehre*. The question naturally arises, and was put to Heidegger, as to when he would explicitate the human aspect of this dimension of Being. The question is serious for, depending on how one reads Heidegger, such an explicitation (as would be "humanism" and "ethics") either has been impossible due to the very nature of the subordination of man in this approach, or it has simply been felt to be unnecessary and thus bracketed in view of the more important question of *first* laying out the basis for an "ontology" or, finally, it is seen as a proper question awaiting the proper time for its development... which presumably should be now. These three interpretations are all well represented in the literature. Heidegger now takes the opportunity to refute the first whose implicit allegation is one of anti-humanism.

[HB, 19]

"Insofern ist das Denken in "Sein und Zeit" gegen den Humanismus" — that thinking is against humanism only insofar as humanistic interpretations do not allow the experiencing of the true worth and dignity of man ("die eigentliche Würde"). But what does Heidegger mean here by experience — "erfahren" ? We would imagine an experience that leads one to make a breakthrough in favor of the real possibilities of a humanism that discovers, develops and respects the dignity of man. But what is this experience ? Presumably the same one as the "Wesenserfahrung" (p. 18): the experience of realizing what it means to say that man is in so far as he eksists ("dass der Mensch ist, indem er eksistiert"). Lest, however, we think that this is unambiguous, especially without considering ek-sistence as the correlative to the "Anspruch des Seins" within the event, we must not forget the open-ended question on what is "wirklich".

Be that as it may, Heidegger formally denies the charge of anti-humanism while necessarily leaving intact, in our analysis, the further question of whether this denial can carry a real historical weight. The intention is certainly admirable: his opposition to humanism is based on the fact that the humanity of man has been sold short through such a metaphysic, i.e., Heidegger's own interpretation of the history of metaphysics.

Positively, he insists that man is "vielmehr *vom* Sein selbst in die Wahrheit des Seins *'geworfen'*, dass er, dergestalt eksistierend, die Wahrheit des Seins *hüte,* damit im Lichte des Seins das Seiende als das Seiende, das es ist, erscheine". It appears that this proposition should be the basis of humanism as determined by the purposeful rôle of man "according to his essence". It is here that some even see the basis of a new humanism in terms of a new theory of participation. This, in fact, may be implied but it would be hard to justify. Firstly, Heidegger rejects "participation" even more than "humanism"...

but again we have the problem of getting beyond the formal denial of the word-concept; secondly, a notion of participation would require that there is to be found in this philosophy a participative and creative rôle for man — and this indeed is one of the most abstruse points in Heidegger even in regard as to its very possibility. However, what is clear from the passage at hand is that man is *somehow* THERE in order to be "there" *so that* being, things — the non-human — may appear as they are... "in the light of Being". This is reminiscent of his notion that man is there so that History may take place. Such a view is now taken up again in terms of the *Kehre:* History does not depend on man because "Die Ankunft des Seienden beruht im *Geschick* des Seins". Hence, as man is no longer to be thought as master of beings but as the one who shepherds them to language and to Being [and thus "participates" — this would be the argument] because he is *the* shepherd of Being, so too he is not the master of history but, it would seem, its shepherd. For "die Ankunft des *Seienden* is really a function of the advent of *Being*.

On the other hand, if the histori*cal* event rests upon the mittance of Being, the question remains whether man "finds the 'com-mitment' (Schickliche) of his essence *as* corresponding to this destiny" [or "mittance", Geschick]. For according to this destiny he must, "as the ek-sistent, watch over and guard the truth".[5] One must note carefully that the very order in which the "remaining question" comes up belies a certain meta-historic point of view favoring another form of meta-humanism. If one should counter that this is not a probable implication of the analysis because of the correlative nature of the thought involved, then there is the suspicion that instead of dealing with an historical event we are in a purely histo*rial*, one-dimensional set-up which invites anew the difficulties of the structuralist interpretation.

---

[5] Für den Menschen aber bleibt die Frage, ob er das Schickliche seines Wesens findet, das diesem Geschick entspricht; denn diesem *gemäss* hat er als der Ek-sistierende die Wahrheit des Seins zu hüten.

[HB, 21]

But what is meant by the conformity alluded to above? "According to [its historico-ontological] essence, language is the house of Being. Thus one is to think the essence of language out of the correspondence *to* Being and indeed as this very correspondance, i.e., the lodging of man's essence."[6] The way, then, that one is to reach some idea of how his essence is in conformity with the historical mittance of Being is knowing what it means to exist through the experience of language — and this would be a "norm", as it were, for the authentic actualization of man's humanity. For the essence of language *is* this correspondence which in turn is the "lodging" of the essence of man. In other words, language as the house of Being is where man is to dwell in order to ek-sist. In this house is given or is e-mitted [cf. "Schickung"] Being such that this very "act" constitutes the historic event which becomes also the true opening of man's humanity: it becomes his historico-historial dwelling! This, therefore, should be the basis of humanism and it is precisely what "humanism" has obscured. For the metaphysical interpretation of "humanitas" [des homo *animalis*] has completely screened out thinking on the real nature of language as "Entsprechung", "Behausung", "Haus", etc.

If this be the case, it seems we might go a long way by comparing the notions of ek-sistence, language and essence (*seinsgechichtlich*) with "entsprechen" as previously discussed. However, this is certainly outside the scope of our "introduction" but it is within our purview to point out some oversimplifications that should not be done — in view of the fact that they have occurred. The "solution" cannot be had according to a simple "logic". We are sure Heidegger would re-echo this loudly. We cannot go back, or even forward in his work, in order to work out by some substitution method an inference

---

[6] Diesem gemäss ist die Sprache das vom Sein ereignete und aus ihm durchfügte Haus des Seins. Daher gilt es, das Wesen der Sprache aus der *Entsprechung* zum Sein und zwar *als* diese Entsprechung, das ist als Behausung des Menschenwesens zu denken.

as to the true meaning of *Entsprechung.* Heidegger does not speak in mere "words"; his universe of discourse shifts because there is no universal discourse possible to tackle the quesion with which he grapples. Thus, any attempt at simply substituting (e.g., "correspondence" and "replying nature", "language", "lodging", "dwelling", etc.) does not work insofar as it leaves behind the particular sphere of the discourse.

[HB, 22]

Humanism is once again explicitly rejected "insofar as it thinks metaphysically". A specific form is especially singled out, that of Jean-Paul Sartre. Sartre's fundamental failure in overcoming metaphysical thinking is manifest in his substitution of one metaphysical proposition by another suffering the same fate. Heidegger is particularly pained at any thought of a confusion with his own work since this would be tantamount to crass anthropologism. Turning Sartre's interpretation that we are moving on a plane where there are only men, Heidegger says: "précisément nous sommes sur un plan où il y a principalement l'Etre". The word "principally" has unfortunately often been overlooked or unevaluated by commentators. It in fact re-establishes an equilibrium of ambiguity as it is followed by: "L'Etre et le plan sind das Selbe".

The entire thrust of his argument is the nature of foundational thinking. It would seem to be difficult to argue that this would not be a valid approach in principle. Nevertheless, there is a serious question that arises on the methodological priority given: "Aber weil das Denken dahin *erst* gelangen soll, das Sein in seiner Wahrheit zu sagen, statt es wie ein Seiendes aus Seiendem zu erklären,...". This may make impossible the whole task as we have already implied but in any event it is Heidegger's chosen priority in establishing what "humanism" is, or should be.

[HB, 26]

We have seen that Heidegger had associated himself with Hölderlin in proclaiming an historical exception to "metaphysical humanism". It is therefore of no little consequence to notice carefully the re-entry on the scene of this poet. For here is also to be found an important indication of how Heidegger intends to find, or at least to point to, a humanism of a new "dimension" ("Damit wir Heutigen jedoch in die Dimension... HB, 18, *supra*).

"Being as destiny emits truth which remains hidden." How then are we to know it? How are we to get at this *Dimension*? Although such a question is not expressed, it seems that the continuation of the text should be read as an "answer": "Aber das Weltgeschick kündigt sich in der *Dichtung* an...". Whereupon we come again upon the name of Hölderlin. We would not be too far afield if we read instead "Heidegger". Hölderlin's thought is held to be more essential, more original and originating and, thus, something other than some Greek neohumanism. After such a promising debut Heidegger drops the subject of poetry! He turns to a renewed criticism of Marx, Sartre, Hegel... What has happened?

The hint is quite clear from the "unsaid" signified by the context of the Letter. Within the positive setting of overcoming metaphysics, humanism is too specific an attitude to stand upon the ground of the *wesentlicher,* unless this humanism is so basic as not to be identifiable with any part of any particular humanism. Heidegger intends to point to that dimension of humanity which went before us and is still in front of us. He must turn to the poetic utterance. For, as he indicates here, there can be no question of thinking man in such a way as to correct, add, or substract from, "traditional" concepts. One must think "ursprünglicher, wesentlicher". Who does this? Hölderlin, for one. And, Heidegger — presumably. How can our author do it? As the poet himself: point to the meta-metaphysical humanism through the poetic (cf. HB, 43), which indeed is, we believe, the major endeavor of his later thought.

Whence comes the crucial question: what sort of humanism could this possibly be? We know of Heidegger's famous statement to be made elsewhere: the poet names the holy. This however is an essential connection which he does not make here. While not alluding to the poetic, he will, nevertheless, return to the idea of the holy and place it in a passage which is perhaps the most commented upon of the entire Letter, sc., the "modus procedendi" from beings, to Being and the holy (pp. 36-7). But this is precisely the furthest point that he can go, or at least cares to indicate: the holy and through the holy to God knows what! Since this is apparently the full thrust of his intention and since this would be the "fulness" of the *Dimension*, then humanity (along with "humanism" in the new dimension) is to be defined and worked out in terms of this same order. We must recall, however, that this is especially clear through his thought expressed in 1949 onward. Though we maintain that it is the trust of the Letter, it also brings us out of the framework of this present introduction and we cannot, consequently, explicitate this, which we have, in any event, done elsewhere [7].

It is exactly at this point that Heidegger re-introduces the question with the comment: "the question you ask helps to clarify the way". This is evidently a great compliment to the writer but one must also recall that he can penetrate just about any question and bring it about that it will clarify the "way". Still, at this juncture in Heidegger's historical development, this particular question has a special appeal. It allows him to reaffirm his interest as primarily a questioning on Being and at the same time to insist that this not only does not derogate from man but that it is the key to getting on the road to asking what humanity is all about.

The question, of course, is "Comment *redonner* un sens au *mot* 'humanisme'?". Heidegger justly remarks that the question supposes a willingness to retain the word and an admission that it has lost [some of] its meaning or sense. But we should also remark — and this is the purpose of our underlining in the question — that this format fits perfectly with his technique: "re-" invites the method of *wieder-holen*; "mot" welcomes the *Sprachanalyse*, etc. We are truly *unterwegs*. It is not too difficult to imagine that this very formulation at the outset of the Letter proved to be the irresistable difference for

---

[7] *Op. cit.*, pp. 297 ff., 330 ff.

launching off, at the moment he did, on the subject of humanism. Certainly we may say that his seizing a question *qua* question coupled with the technique of re-retrieving the sense of a word does not by itself justify any special argumentation for interpreting the Letter. For this is his overall manner, one that should be judged elsewhere. More important is the opportunity to strike a balance on the question of the man-Being relationship. We state nothing startling. Nor need we in order to avoid unfortunate oversimplifications of some commentators.

Heidegger's immediate comment on the question comes as no surprise. The meaning has been lost through its "metaphysical essence" but our questioning has brought us to penetrate the essence of humanism and thus to think more orginally the essence of man. There is, consequently, the possibility to give back to the *word* "humanism" an historic sense ("...in das fragwürdige Wesen des Humanismus fürht,... das Wesen des Menschen anfänglicher zu denken. ...einen geschichtlichen Sinn zurückzugeben"). As for the word "humanism", its component parts suggest "humanitas" (for "humanum") and "Wesen" (for "ismus"). But going beyond the word to give back its meaning can be done only through determining and recapturing anew its sense ("wiederbestimmen").

This last point invites the author to bring to bear his entire method. For this "wiederbestimmen" requires that we "experience" more originally the essence of man ["anfänglicher zu erfahren"]. This in turn will mean coming to the experience, or at least preparing for it and pointing to it, through his unique mixture of questioning, etymologizing, and historicizing that constitutes Heideggerian "hermeneutics". It is thus that the Letter, as we shall see, will move through a consideration of language, ethos, dwelling and Being.

This entire process is already implied when the term "humanism", if one decides to retain it, means: "the essence of man is essential for the truth of Being such that from now on it is not man uniquely as such that matters". It is then Being in relation to man that, in terms of man's place in the "world", asks the question which is not only *geschichtlich* but also *geschicklich*... "in seiner Weise geschicklich". Finally Heidegger admits that he is thinking of a strange sort of "humanism", a word which is "lucus a non lucendo". This most enigmatic closing of the passage says a great deal only in terms of his whole philosophy which is clearly far beyond the scope of this introduction. We dare suggest, however, that the reader would find a rewarding, or at least a stimulating, reflection through a comparative reading of J. Gonda's article "Wereld en hemel in de Veda" (no. 72)*. We make an exception in adding this work to our complementary bibliography for two reasons: it is well known that Heidegger is no stranger to Eastern thought; it is scarcely known that commentators do not illucidate this saying [8].

[HB, 32]

"Should one still call 'humanism' this thought which speaks out against all prior humanism without, however, being at all the spokesman of the inhuman?". An honest question. By throwing out the word, it would have been easier to think out afresh the "humanitas of homo humanus"; on the other hand, one would like to retain the word in at least an initial effort at communication and a linking up with a certain amount of tradition. But if Heidegger drops this word, just as he eventually abandoned "metaphysics" and "ontology", he might open his thought to what he calls essential misunderstanding (e.g., anti-humanism, nihilism, irrationalism). Indeed, we shall see that after some ten pages of toying with this idea, there is

---

* Numbers refer to the bibliography.

[8] About the closest we come to is Krüger (no. 35a, p. 164): "Heideggers Humanismus ist ja ein "lucus a non lucendo". Aber die übermenschliche und übergöttliche Wahrheit ek-sistiert doch, wie sich zeigte, nur geschichtlich im Menschen, und insofern ist Heideggers Lehre auch wieder "Humanismus im äussersten Sinn". On the contrary to suggest only the most striking parallels in Gonda: the idea of place is not limited to space; the ideas of "bewoning" and "nabijheid" are key ones of HB ("Bewohnung", "Nähe"); the play on "woods-place-light" (locus-lux) is found in Heidegger and ties in with Being as concealing-revealing by the historical nature of its manifestation.

implied a parallel: "ontology" had to be abandoned in the effort of a "fundamental ontology", so too "humanism" is to be abandoned in view of a ... "fundamental humanism"? — Heidegger does not make the same mistake twice: "fundamental humanism" as a word-concept is never explicitated, we pass on to *ethos*, just as "fundamental ontology" explicitly gives way to the poetic.

But first Heidegger is going to explicitate the "logic" of an inapplicable logic to his own thought in an effort to show how so many interpreters have mistaken his tactical target for his overall strategy. And this he must do with care, for there is otherwise no reason to believe that his present thought on humanism would suffer a different fate, since, in the past, his own formal denials have not always had consistent credence. Hence, he must expose this because his "logic" does remain identical: if he attacked the thinking about beings as obscuring that about Being, so he must do likewise on the thinking about humanism that has hidden the humanity of man; if metaphysics led to forgetting Being so also humanism forgets the essence of man in that very "dimension" where man has his home.

Can one then ask legitimately of Heidegger what happens to the being of man [cf. HB, 30; *supra*, p. 41] when his first concern is asking about Being? Any negative critique must be able to enter at some point into Heidegger's own discourse. No purely extrinsic logic will do, especially if it has some aprioristic content or some conceptual forms calling for their opposites. Perhaps Heidegger's reasoning is reminiscent of Brutus' "not that I loved Caesar less but Rome more": not that he considers man less but Being more — perhaps. In any case, he summarizes (pp. 32-4) a false logic as a catalogue of sins, as it were, against his own thought: by being against "humanism", one is not (necessarily) for barbarism and the inhuman; by attacking "logic", one is not (necessarily) favoring illogism and irrationalism; by thinking against "values", one does not necessarily announce everything as valueless; by opting for man as "Being-in-the-world", one does not thereby affirm a positivism or a refusal of all "transcendence"; by referring to

Nietzsche's "death of God", one does not (necessarily) hold for atheism or a godless man; because this philosophy goes against what humanity holds as great and sacred, it does not propose nihilism; thus, opposition to humanism is by no means a defense of the inhuman but *opens up new perspectives*.

We have resummarized this catalogue because it is not to be taken as some idle classification. Any commentator of his thought or any thinker who claims a positive influence from this thought cannot ignore these assertions. If, nevertheless, one maintains that in fact Heidegger is still open to such charges — and they are representatives to affirm each one of them even after their publication — all well and good, provided he respects some basic norms of criticism (cf. p. 17).

If, for example, one agrees with Heidegger that he has not done an anthropology, then one cannot accuse him of anti-humanism in any ordinary sense of the word. For then his thought is precisely "sur ce plan" where one cannot directly make such a predication. On the other hand, it seems that this reasoning favors a meta-humanism. Now, within this latter framework it is possible that one may be able to show that Heidegger has effectively posited a vacuous man with a consequent "anti-humanism". Such a type of anti-humanism could be compatable within the primary affirmation of a meta-humanism. For it is of a different type than what one usually ascribes and would be intelligible within the *Zusammenhang* of Heideggerian thought. Then, if one were willing to go further by asserting that due to such an "objective" derogation, his thought is radically inconsistent, incoherent, insubstantial, then such a critique would have to show that this is no mere prolongation of some abstract logic, a device all too easily turned into a rhetorical reduction to absurdity. To attempt a valid, penetrating reduction may well be possible but it would be no easy ask. For according to the classic principle that man can only find and formulate that certitude which is compatable with the matter on hand and warranted by it, one wonders how many levels of Heidegger's thought are really so penetrable as to elicit a clearly ordered analysis. We suspect at times that we have on these pages a plea that would close so many doors to an easy critique as to put the critic at a seriously disadvantaged position. For he can then be "refuted" for applying a logic. Nevertheless, the true philosophical critique, as logical as it may be, need not fall victim to the charge of merely applying a critique *to* a thought. Yet, it is not too surprising that the percentage of valid criticisms of Heidegger is not overwhelming.

Not only would it be possible to speak of an anti-humanism within a meta-humanism, it may still be possible that, inspite of Brutus, Heidegger has "killed" man in another way. We have already seen the difficulties of following the procedure whereby he wishes to clarify the state of Being "before" that of man; this approach, as well as that of the negative moment of overcoming metaphysicis, can lead to a factual anti-humanism that closer examination would reveal as a "de-humanism" (*Enthumanismus*) rather than a mere anti-humanism. This possibility appeares from a few indications gleaned from the next pages.

[HB, 34/5]

The question of value is rightly felt as needing a particular explicitation and, as far as we are concerned, it has the advantage of leading us into the unity of Heidegger's method.

Thinking that goes against "values" does not claim that "culture", "dignity" of man, and "God" are valueless. On the contrary, value considerations are precisely what robs these of their dignity (just as "humanism" has done so in regard to man such that a new approach is required to restore his dignity, HB, 31). "Value" considerations are subjectivizations. Proclaiming God as the highest value degrades his essence and the humanistic setting up of man as value (and even more so as *the* value) would be no less derogating and derogatory.

The process of subjectivization is one of objectification and, hence, of cleaving, splitting and opposing. Thus, for example, a Christian or theological understanding of Heidegger's notion of humanity as Being-in-the-world posited a forsaken man, isolated from the transcendent [compare HB, 21]. This interpretation turned Heidegger's concept into man as "lediglich ein 'weltliches' Wesen" — which is exactly what he ascribes to the pernicious influence of humanism ("Menschen, lediglich als solchen", HB, 31). On the contrary, "Thinking against values means: against subjectivizing beings [reducing them] to a pure object [and being in favor of] bringing before thought the lighting-up process of the truth of Being".

What does all this mean for the method and unity that underlies Heidegger's approach to the question of Humanism ? Subjectivization is a subject-object opposition which constitutes an integral part of metaphysical and onto-theological thinking. To recapture not only the perspective of the question of Being but also that of man and of even the possibility of asking about God, one comes to a process of *Ensubjektivierung* which has two concomitant moments: de-divinization [*Ent-Götterung*] and "de-humanization". These moments fall into one process: the question of man within the world as opposed to another "world", of man as destined for another "world" implying an opposition of some sort with Being-in-the-world, of man in relation to the Transcendent or not — the hardened ground of all these false oppositions, outcroppings grown before the ground was prepared for the sowing of such questions, must be turned over and overturned as part of the the one and the same procedure according to Heidegger's *Denkweg*.

[HB, 36]

Man is not only not a "wordly" being in contradistinction to some "spiritual" world but "the proposition, the essence of man consists in Being-in-the-world, resolves nothing on whether man in the metaphysico-theological sense, is a being only of this world or the other" ("ein nur diesseitiges oder ob er ein jenseitiges Wesen sei"). But in Heidegger's thought man is neither for nor against the "other" world, just as his thinking is neither theistic nor athetistic and, as further on in the Letter, his ethical thought is neither practical nor theoretical. This is an aspect of the overcoming method: his thought is neither theistic nor atheistic just as it must necessarily be neither humanistic nor a-humanistic. These are two, paired moments of the same process. In itself this presents no problem, in fact it may have a certain appeal. The question remains, however, and it is a serious one: if we grant that Heidegger's *thought* (and not just his method) is so fundamental as to escape all these "categories" and as not even to favor any one of them, can it exist? Can it become a concrete, historical expression? Or is it merely some structuralist form? The irony would not be missing: a meta-metaphysical structuralism. Without exactly putting it this way, more than one interpreter has opted along these lines.

To give Heidegger his due, one must admit that the structuralist view, being of its very nature a "stricter science" than that admitted by the nature of philosophy itself, fosters, if it is not indeed at first encouraged by, a "neutralist" view. An inbred detachment and indifferentism seem quite incompatible with our author's intention and only superficially compatible with the method influenced by the bracketing approach. Furthermore, Heidegger would argue that he is precisely in no framework, let alone a structuralist one for the simple reason that he has refused to set off any arbitrary limits to the implication of his thinking. An this must be taken seriously in any evaluation of this thought even if such an affirmation does not necessarily absolve one from a factual structuring. Heidegger's argument is that whatever limit there may be to thought is not to be set by man, but by Being [9]. Thus the limits of such thinking, as we continue with the text (p. 37) consists in a type of givenness due to the very way the truth of Being gives itself

---

[9] This principle applies also to language, cf. HB, 10 (cited, p. 30). We find here the link between "de-divinization" and "de-humanization" (pp. 40 and 53, above). It is man's language that closes off the revealing-process; it is his language that "kills", not Being's. In so doing, man withers away, shut up in a "humanism" cut off from the historic dwelling which is Being's language. Thus, for Heidegger, man must wait. He must wait for the proper *seinsgeschichtlich* expression. Therefore, the thrust of Heidegger's thought is expressed in the passage "Erst aus der Wahrheit des Seins... was das Wort 'Gott' nennen soll" (36/7) which we have characterized (p. 47) as a "modus procedendi" and which we shall further examine at the end of part III.

and comes-into-presence as that which is to be thought. Therefore, it is not out of indifferentism nor out of any arbitrary cut off point that his philosophical approach is such in reference to theism, humanism and values but "aus der Achtung der *Grenzen*, die dem Denken als Denken gesetzt sind und zwar durch das, was sich ihm als das Zu-denkende gibt, durch die Wahrheit des Seins".

[HB, 37f]

We now come upon an explicit identification within the Heideggerian approach. What is meant by "overcoming" [überwinden] ? It is the act of "zurücksteigen". A going back down to the "proximity of Being". This much was expected in view of our elaboration of the notion contained in the very question: "Comment *redonner*... ?". Now, for what purpose does he want to attempt such a re-descent ? In order to be able to think the truth of Being which act is going to be at the same time, by virtue of the simultaneity of the two moments already spoken about, the authentic thinking of humanity: "Die Wahrheit des Seins denken, heisst *zugleich*: die humanitas des homo humanus denken". Thus we have *an* identity of means and "object". And if we ask for a further explicitation, he will tell us: "Das Denken geleitet die geschichtliche Eksistenz, das heisst die humanitas des homo humanus, in den Bereich des Aufgangs des Heilen" (p. 43).

But this beautiful picture is somewhat marred. That word "*geleitet*". How much weight should be given to it ? After seriously doubting the validity of an overall charge of "structuralism" we fall back into the suspicion that man is "one" who is "subordinated" and *led*, if not determined, by some pregivenness of language such that his word cannot become truly his own (*eigent*lich).

This same suspicion is reinforced by the very sentence added to terminate the passage (sc., "zugleich") that we have just seen: "Es gilt die Humanitas, *zu diensten* der Wahrheit des Seins, aber ohne den Humanismus in metaphysischen Sinne". This somewhat picturesque expression, "to be at the service of truth", is in effect translatable, by those who see a structuralist connotation in terms of the whole movement of Heidegger's thought, as "in the servitude of truth". For what service can man bring but to be simply there as a service-attendant [10].

Let us note the nature of the earlier statement since it opens the Letter to a consideration of its next question. "Thinking the truth of Being is the thinking at the same time of the humanitas of homo humanus». Why is such a coïncidence had ? It happens when humanity is at the service of truth, to which it is already in fundamental rapport. This is the condition for the coïncidence: it will be identified with Heidegger's conception of *sprechen* (HB, 45-47). The supposition is explicit: "humanism" is not to be taken in the metaphysical sense. But positively, in view of the nature of the language analysis, it will be difficult to avoid some connotation of the structuralist by reason of this happy harmony.

[HB, 38]

The question opened by these last remarks is one that has long been expected: "if humanity is so essentially focused in view of the thinking of Being, must not "ontology" then be completed by "ethics" ?". We see, at least in principle, the inescapable coupling of the question of Being, of man, and of a fundamental relation of "action" (HB, 5): a *Grundethik*.

The answer is well known: he rejects the question framed in terms of disciplines, sc., "ontology" and "ethics". No need to pause here. More important is his contention that he is on a fundamental level prior to such distinctions. Here is the attempt to discover the link between a pre-ontology and a pre-ethic, in one and the same fundamental ground.

For this purpose, he already has the elements: the ideas of "throwness", "call", "project", etc. prior to any systematic elaboration of throught or any arbitrarily marked off scientific

---

[10] Thus, as we have analyzed elsewhere, man would be one whose presence symbolizes, without really effecting it in some way, the relation which is the truth of Being. He would be merely a witness who is a passive stand-in, a "Platzhalter". Cf. *op. cit.*, p. 295.

discipline. These factors are *joined* and *conjoined* in the originative unity of language: the addressing and demanding word, the emittance of language as destiny and history, the bringing to language of what is already in Being's relation and finally the essenc-ing of all this as thought, sc. as "l'engagement par l'Etre et pour l'Etre" (HB, 5). Therefore, the question of ethics is really put in terms of the very first page of this Letter. It is to be posited according to the interior relationship of the "in den Anspruch nehmen" so that one may see what this "engagement" is... a natural fulfilment of an originative relation which already is. This then is the "ethical" question: the manner in which the originally *joined* relation within the relation of Being to man becomes a *conjoined* way for man to "dwell on this earth" [11].

Let us return briefly and more closely to the text in order to clarify some areas of further conflicting interpretations and in order to summarize a shift of terminology underlining the author's movement through his notion of "humanism" and to stress at the same time his fundamental approach to the question in terms of the context of his general philosophy.

[HB, 38]

Out of the fundamental relationship of the essence of man to Being, Heidegger recognizes the importance of ethics from the need of standing, according to some originating directives, within the historical destiny which Being emits to man. Naturally we ask how Heidegger expects man to be able to do this. He can answer in accordance with our note below that he is (supposedly) on the most basic level of an ethic where somehow will come forth *man's ethos as Being's wayfarer*. But this

---

[11] Thus, HB, 41: "Soll nun gemäss der Grundbedeutung des Wortes êthos der Name Ethik dies sagen, dass sie den Aufenthalt des Menschen bedenkt, dann ist *dasjenige* Denken, das die Wahrheit des Seins als das anfängliche Element des Menschen als eines eksistierenden denkt, *in sich schon* die ursprüngliche Ethik». Ergo, on the basis of this basic level: "Das Tun des Denkens [harking back to p. 5] ist weder theoretisch noch praktisch, noch ist es die Verkoppelung beider Verhaltungsweisen" (46).

must somehow be "filled" by experience. And here we return to the fundamental ambiguity in Heidegger that must be preserved pending a complete and intrinsic analysis of the question: if we do not turn to an existentiel experiencing, how will this ethos ever be filled out? If we do, is this basically compatable with the way his thought has turned out? Certainly, we cannot make him out to be a blatant existentialist. His reference to "experiencing man" cannot be divorced from our earlier difficulties with the term "erfahren". Nevertheless, this entire passage, just to take the example of its English translation, is given an unjustified twist, as do many other commentators [12].

[HB, 41/2]

That thinking which is a fundamental and original ethic is not so because it is ontology; for, as Heidegger explains, ontology is without its fundament because it thinks only beings and not the truth of Being. Moreover, the experience of *Sein und Zeit* has been that the very word ontology leads people astray inspite of the professed effort to get at fundamental and foundational thought. While redeveloping this theme, he intertwines its complement in terms of *êthos*. In our opinion this represents most closely the thinking he was searching to express.

Ethos is sojourning ("Aufenthalt") in the openness of

---

[12] "Letter on Humanism", translated by Edgar LOHNER, in *Philosophy of the Twentieth Century*, ed. W. Barrett *et al.*, New York, Random House, 1962, vol. III, p. 295 [HB, 38]: "... there the desire must arise for personally relevant directives", this renders the "neutral" text: "... muss das Verlangen nach einer verbindlichen Anweisung erwachen". The next paragraph gives: "But does this crisis ever absolve thought of the responsibility [sic] of thinking...", a gratuitous addition to "Aber entbindet diese Not je das Denken davon...". This personalization of the text is by no means an isolated example; indeed, back on p. 281 [HB, 19] he does so as to contradict the author's thought: "For man, however, the question remains whether he finds what is appropriate to his essence to correspond to his destiny; according to this, as an ex-sisting person [sic], he has to guard the truth of Being".

Being and "in die Wahrheit des Seins". But is not this "action" on the same plane as the thought "that questions after the truth of Being and by that very fact determines the essential sojourn of man from and towards Being" — the same thought that is neither ethics nor ontology ? Thus the fundament, which "Fundamentalontologie" had sought by thinking "in the truth of Being", *ethos* would discover it by standing in the truth, eksisting and dwelling in it, such that "this dwelling is the essence of Being-in-the-world".

We may infer that thinking and dwelling in the truth of Being belong to the ethos-connective of pre-ontology and pre-ethics already mentioned. If this is the essence of the "geschichtliche Eksistenz, das heisst die humanistas des homo humanus" (43), ethos would be the "ursprüngliche Grundethik" which is neither theoretical nor practical for the same reason that Heidegger's previous thought expressed as Being-in-the-world is neither theistic nor atheistic. "Ethos" means this: *menschlich wohnen,* that is, dwelling essentially as *homo humanus.*

Such a fundamental ethos sidesteps the question of elaborating any rules or directives of behavior. If one should ask *how* man can "menschlich wohnen", the answer would be "dichterisch wohnen" (43). Now, this answer says philosophically a great deal or quasi nothing according to a radical divergence of opinion as to the poetic and its function in Heidegger in particular.

What has happened here to the development of Heidegger's theme, indeed, to the *Zusammenhang* of his thought ? The word "humanism" drops out. True, "humanitas" reappears but this is not the principal affirmation. Just as he had to drop "ontology" because people insisted (as he claims) on thinking only beings, so also "humanism" which leads merely to a thinking of man as such. But both these terms are positively incorporated through the development of one idea: *ethos.* Indeed, the title of the Letter could well have been "On Ethos" since "Humanismus" (without its "metaphysical meaning") *is,* in the last analysis, the ethos of man (homo humanus). Ethos, in its various aspects alluded to in the Letter, will dominate the rest of Heideggerian thought, e.g., "wohnen" with "Haus des Seins/der Sprache" and "aufenthalten" with being "underway to language". This fact alone would justify further effort at the Letter's interpretation.

Taking note of the argument (41/2) in which Heidegger "apologizes" for having used the term "ontology" (and all metaphysical language), we see more clearly that it was a start at communication within a certain framework and an attempt at the same time to point outside its restrictions, so too it seems that the same thing could be said for the *word* "humanism": the Letter is in reality a "repetition" of the entire twenty year process since *Sein und Zeit,* a repetition under one aspect which is still the whole, since it represents the "essence of essential (or foundational) thinking". We understand this process as a movement from "humanism" to "humanitas", then to "Eksistenz", and on to *êthos,* and from there to "wohnen", "Offenheit", "Behausung" and (45, 47) "Sprache"; these latter aspects all being rooted in the fundamental notion of the essence of ethos.

Does this repetition by Heidegger of himself communicate more than the original? Certainly it is more poetical. But a close examination, which is evidently outside the scope of this presentation of the critical opinions on "humanism" and "ethics", would show that the original ambiguities remain no less fundamental and that they may well have been compounded through the elaboration of an ethos of and in language, an ethos in and of the Logos.

Let us return briefly to some of the questions. In what sense does the Letter and the "new humanism" allow for experience? Is "speaking" a real human endeavor? "Who" is communicating? What is the relation of the question of humanism with that of the *Kehre*? Does the post-reversal development promise more for a humanism than did *Sein und Zeit?* Heidegger would say that thinking along the lines of "homo humanus" and of "êthos" avoids the temptation of thinking of man "als solche" and "lediglich". No doubt. But can we think man "aus" Being? And no matter what may be the outcome of all this, can we allow for man's creative potentialities essential to any humanism? Though it is not according to Heidegger's intention, man may well be in fact so utterly subordinated as to render historical man impossible; moreover, it may well be Heidegger's intention that he is so "co-ordinated" that his action is merely that of a correlative "Entsprechung". This of couse would smack of "meta-structuralist" thought. To clarify or to do away with such serious suspicions requires that we have a better understanding at least of what he means by "experience". And this point is perhaps impossible to resolve. It is not a hermeneutic cercle. It represents a fundamental doubt arising out of a fundamental ambiguity. It is quite possible that Heidegger deliberately intends to maintain things this way. And he may be right, for after all, strict logic is not ambiguous, nor is it philosophy. But there is a limit. A limit that man and not "Being" places if one wishes to communicate. In the final analysis, "humanism" for Heidegger (not the word!) means dwelling in this world poetically and thus in the lighting-up process that opens on the "Dimension" of authentic man and opens new perspectives to humanism. This means, as we have in effect tried to show through this reading, that Heidegger's thought, both as ultimately intended and as actually and factually developed, contains a more ample core of ambiguity than most philosophical thought. This fact must be respected in any interpretation of the Letter; correlatively, any facile, clear cut critique would be, at least on this score, initially suspect. Finally, at the end of our next section, this ambiguity will return as the question of the symbolic.

A NOTE ON THE ENGLISH TRANSLATION

Perhaps a contributing factor to the paucity of material in English on the very questions proposed by the Letter is the firm evidence, provided by the Lohner translation, of its inherent difficulties complicated by the lack of a minimal convention among English translations and, in this case, by the absence of some notice for those conventions that are adopted

— the reader will have noticed that we have used wherever feasible Richardson's vocabulary (no. 47a). In this brief comment upon this translation to complement our previous remarks (cf. note, p. 58, where the edition is also given), we cannot be but negative to forewarn the reader who may wish to depend upon it to some extent. This is an unfortunate and unpleasant task but it is a duty. The following remarks are only a sampling in order to give an unmistakable indication of the deplorable quality of this rendition; our critical severity is in fact unmatched by the distressingly overpowering evidence.

It is true that one may not object to a coloring of the text as an inherent part of the translating process but the reader should at least be warned when no limits are imposed to this undertaking. To translate "Die Denkenden und Dichtenden" of the first page by "Whoever thinks or creates in words" is certainly at the limit of the translator's liberty but to supply the word "creature" in the expression "ein jenseitiges Wesen" (HB, 36; trsl., 293) or to turn "als der Ek-sistierende" — and there is no more to the phrase (cf. note. p. 58) — into "as an ex-sisting person", presumably for the sake of readability, is unpardonable, especially without a note explaining the radical inconsistancy of thought.

There is no need to go into omissions and additions to the text. Let us take page 45 (trsl., 300) to bring out three pertinent points: a) an unwarranted personalist nuance compounded with an inconsistent rendition, b) a negation of the significance of the author's idea of thought, c) a fundamental negation of the relative rôle of thought (and of man) in reference to Being.

"Das Geringe", insignificance", is rendered as "humbleness"; then, "dieses *unscheinbare* Tun des Denkens" is itself rendered as "this insignificant act". "Dieses Ankommende bringt das ek-sistierende Denken seinerseits in seinem Sagen zur Sprache" is translated *exactly* as follows: "As it [Being] arrives, it [Being] in its turn brings ex-sisting thought to language in its telling". True, if the first six words are taken as *isolated,* the text allows us to read either subject-verb-object or object-verb-subject. But in fact, *Denken* is the only subject possible: 1) as to the sentence, "seinerseits" is meant to imply something; 2) as to the paragraph, it is a carefully structured balance: Denken bringt..., Sein kommt... (and, "seinerseits") Denken bringt...; 3) as to the context of Heidegger's thought, it would otherwise be a fundamental negation because this is the central notion of *entsprechen,* it is the idea of history where *Denken, seinerseits ist Da;* when Being comes to language, man is there, so that according to his essence, beings may come to language and to Being.

But then, this very distinction is left completely without foundation in the translation of the Letter for the very outset contains two fundamental errors: a) SEIN is rendered once as "Being", another time as "what is" (which is then rightly used for "Seiende"), b) *"the relation of Being to* the essence of man" is indifferently equivalent to "man's relation to..." because in both cases the German is identical, namely "den Bezug des Seins zum...". All this betrays the translator's penchant for the "reversal"; in fact it is a habit. To cite one more example: "But if the thought of Being is so essentially focussed on humanitas..." renders "Wenn aber die Humanitas so wesenhaft für das Denken des Seins im Blick steht..." (HB, 38; trsl., 259).

It is painfully clear that it would not be worthwhile to bring further corrections to this rendition. One would have to make anew a translation.

III

THE INTERPRETATIONS OF THE LETTER

The reader will note that the principal, critical bibliography is broken down into four classes of interpretation arbitrarily coded A to D. The letter appearing before each author is intended to facilitate grouping for further research and analysis. Clearly, such a determination must allow considerable span within each "class"; consequently, we have defined them accordingly but we have also attempted to respect the individual authors by shadings within their particular categorization.

Let us first list the most characteristic views and problems underscored by each class; then, examine each one in order to find what common ground, outlook or interest is behind each. A comparison of these classes will highten the "HB-questions" such that we shall have to outline what may be the significance of all this data, or at least, in what sense it is pointing according to the lines of a fundamental problematic which is at once classic and contemporary.

But one must first note very carefully that in listing the characteristics of each class "and" most often signifies "and/or". Furthermore, in the development of each group our statements are not meant to compromise one author in terms of another. We intend rather to give the principal thrust of each group. In stringing together their qualities, we tend to form a "pure case" representing each group but, in fact, few authors would follow us down to the last statement. Most will drop off at a certain point and all will recognize themselves in at least one important point of the category in which they find themselves placed.

A stands for *anti*-humanism, for action that is a-personal and even anti-human in outlook. "Entsprechen" is a type of correspondence, a structure implying a devaluation of man's action and of his being. Man's reality is emptied out; a real history as belonging to him is negated; man is a mere instrument. Correlatively, some discover a determinism, or at least an unduly stressed destiny.

B stands for *meta*-humanism, the meta-historical and overly abstract thought. "Entsprechen" is an ideal, or an idealized eschatology; an unrealistic, if not unreal, position is stressed as a mere schema or detached structure. The meta-historical is mythical; often it is merely mythical, being a way without a door. If the effective absence of man is sufficiently underscored as incompatible, one arrives at class-A, above.

C stands for *authentic* humanism and the truly existentiel. "Entsprechen" means true human activity, dialogue, response or the wherewithal to act while humbly waiting, listening, attending, etc. A type of realism, the manifestation of Being goes with a true realization of man himself. A content is assumed, affirmed or simply seen as existenti*el*, personal, real and participatory action with Being. Heidegger's thought is a way or at least a guide and, as a minimum, a Socratic gadfly to help us find the way.

D represents the unclassified group. The reason is apparent in each particular case. In general, however, it often represents a straddled position or one not immediately relative to the above categories; whenever we have seriously hesitated, we have used "D" while indicating the author's trend.

CLASS-C

It is best to start with an examination of the positive interpretation. A study of the authors representing class-A is facilitated by considering two basic points: the *fundamental approach* or general philosophical attitude that comes into play and the function of the *overcoming-process* ["Überwindung"] manifested at various levels of thought and moments of reasoning. This process which in most generic terms combines the negative and the positive, will be seen in further detail under the negative of class-C, sc., A.

The most striking fact about group-C is the bold simplicity of insight which accounts for — or is the result of — the interpretation of a genuine authenticity and of a profound humanism. Some emphasize "the identity of the Da of Being and man" praising man as Being's instrument [40]*; others insist that man's response is *merely* that of Being and that language is Being's [57], indeed to the point that man is Thinking, rather than man is thinking, when Being thinks [56].

We dare say that most philosophers, at least when not caught up in a flight of insight, would refrain from explicitating such propositions for obvious reasons. Nevertheless, we do suggest that one cannot judge too hastiliy the value of these statements since what may appear naïve to an outsider not apppreciating the insight involved can in fact be but an inadequate expression of the simplicity of the insight, given the fact that truth wears a disarming simplicity. Perhaps this accounts for an apparent unawareness, neglect or sense of unimportance and non-relevancy as regards noetic questions — e.g., whether one is coming to some Hegelian or Fichtean position, or to some sort of idealism in which historical development completely falls outside the hands of man. There is, however, no excuse for the naïve enthusiasm that projects the saying of a philosopher, whether the case be philosophical, ethical, religious or theological [respectively, 36, 15; 41, 27, 58]; nor indeed for those who renounce the task of communicating effectively by not touching upon questions that come to the mind of a reader given even to the briefest moment of serious reflection.

The philosopher does, in a way, what comes naturally but he has the task to do it, if not systematically, at least exensively and intensively: reflect seriously on experience, rethink the obvious and reground the significance of insight. Now, in "returning" to this task as concerns the fundamental attitude

* All numbers in square brackets refer to the authors of the bibliography.

in approaching anything, it clearly involves one's interpretation of a philosopher's thought. What fundamental approach is suggested by group-C?

We find the following as the basic tendency: the "simplicity" of the approach is explained as a dialogue [54] and a poetic [1, 14], or it takes on the connotations of some philosophical faith [40, 46], or it remains a "fidelity" in tune with the real [20]. In some cases, it must be admitted, it is no easy task to differentiate profound insight from mere naïveté.

The other basic point involved, which we use to foster some general appreciation of the climate of class-A, deals not with the fundamental outlook but with its explicitation, or better with the method of working it out. As applied to Heidegger, this point becomes concretely the authors' grasp, explanation, transformation or judgement of the validity of the "overcoming-process". We wish to suggest briefly how this point is a pivot around which turn most of the reasoning and argumentation of an interpreter's analysis of Heidegger — a point, which the reader will recognize as a very classic one redressed by Heidegger. The process is more than his "own" in the sense that it partakes of a fundamental approach of thought found throughout the history of western philosophy and theology. For this reason, it is by no means an arbitrary focal point.

The "Überwindung" consists of a double moment, negative and positive, forming *one* process. That this is Heidegger's view, there is no doubt; whether he has succeeded is an honestly disputable point. If the two moments are not bound together both in their origin and in their development, there is no authentic way to proceed. For one is then left with the negative, which isolated becomes a Nihilism or some form of pessimism; or one is left with some idealized, unperturbed optimism and will-power; or, as is generally the case, one faces two isolated moments that are set for an unresolvable conflict. Therefore, when interpreting Heidegger's thought as either an authentic way or as some mere renewal of Nihilism and pessimism, one must ask whether Heidegger handels successfully both the setting up of the question of "Überwindung" and the method of his follow-through. One must not be carried away by some of Heidegger's forceful insights and claim that ipso facto they are the outcome of his approach. Perhaps they are after all, but a critical interpreter should justify them and not just proclaim — as is too often the case in class-A — that our philosopher is the way.

Around the fact of the "double moment" we many now sketch some of the insights of our C-group authors. We find, for example, the incisive interpretation that the presence of alienation and of homelessness is at once present with a sense of homecoming [18] — though in what sense this is on the lived-level in Heidegger must remain an open question. Such presence is an evident expression of the bi-valent, the positive-negative; moreover, since Being is at once revealing and concealing, then language (and the word) must have the same rôle. One may well hold that language (and for instance the very word "humanism") must be rethought in terms of Being [9, 11], but language itself must have at once both functions of the "double moment"; sc., if it conceals (as an obstacle), it also, and indeed it must for the same fundamental reason, be signi-fying.

On another level, one should maintain that the positive must come out of the negative moment, sc., the *"Destruktion"*, which should exist only as revealing the positive. No sense worrying whether the negative factor is too strongly present [11], if the other has not yet begun to appear. Indeed one must recognize that the process has to open positively [43]. But then, is some form of participation necessary? Indeed, one author is so aware of it that he labels the outcome of this process, precisely as it is found in HB, as a new theory or form of participation [44]. We believe that some such type of recognition is necessary if we are to avoid an emanational position in which the instrument, the voice of Being, etc. fail to become realities with their own rights. In class-C, a form of participation is often affirmed, almost always implied but scarcely ever examined; yet, the question is really unavoidable if a type-C interpretation is to be maintained.

CLASS-A

An examination of representative authors of this class produces the startling impression that the very factors that are praised as "authentic and existentiel" by the prior group are here condemned as Heidegger's clearest difficiencies. We shall see that this impression becomes a sound judgement when the forces at play around the same points are discovered, especially upon examining the fundamental approach that may well be decisive, when we reconsider the crucial text "Erst aus...". Let us first consider briefly the data of class-A by summarizing it under two aspects: the notion of "place" in Heidegger and the argument or the misunderstandings that trash about the key notion of "Überwindung".

Most of the important points underscored by this group can easily be knitted together under the non-univocal idea of "place". The thematic chain to be sketched is no mere knitting trick. Any serious reflection on the important philosophical notion of place would show otherwise; our purpose, however, excludes such developments, especially if already done in large measure [92]. Our purpose is more practically oriented, it is to let the reader move more easily through the literature by giving him a feel of the different global approaches.

Man is the place of revelation. But if he is merely this, a "place", he becomes de-personalized before a non-personal being [13], he is subject to impersonal thought [21]. Surely if it is difficult to find what place man has in the historical process, Heidegger should not reduce his action to that of an instrument [10, 26] since man could no longer open up the sense of Being [37a], nor could he find a real medium of historical encounter [10]; on the other hand, the reality of man does not quite fit into the historical Event [45], whether it is because Heidegger reduces him to a dialectical moment [30], to some phenomenological bracket [50], or to an emptied being [55]. Consequently, even if one should find in Heidegger a meaningful place for the reality which is man, would it still have anything to do with what is essentially man's [2]? Finally, what is the place of man before Being? Heidegger's Being can be read with the attributes of Logos or of God [6]; if man is to stand before such a Being, ethical behavior is a sheer impossibility [7]. In a word, the development of the notion of place opens up upon two correlative critiques: man's action is reduced to some type of instrument, thus his being becomes a puppet on life's stage; Being becomes the overriding reality that dominates *as* thinking, speaking and acting (in and for man), thus Being becomes some overall reality *or* some superstructure mistakingly conceived — the "or" marks the divergence as to whether Heidegger is open to some existentiel dimension or remains purely on the existenti*al* plane.

The second notion around which gravitates the A-class data is the function of "Überwindung". Having already touched upon this under class-C, we may rapidly proceed to the point. The success or failure of this process determines whether or not Heidegger has fallen into an anti-humanism, sc. a de-humanized being and/or the impossibility of having responsible, hence ethical, behavior. For, if the negative moment does not of its very nature open, in the same process, upon the positive, there exists an "anti-position" which cannot be overcome by any intention of the author. Heidegger's *intention* is certainly neither "anti", nor "negative" in the *carefully* nuanced sense of these words [13]; consequently, the question should bear on the intrinsic coherency of his thought, specifically, the "overcoming-process".

If the process does come off, as in Pöggeler's analysis for

---

[13] Let us give one indication of the fuller context of the negative. According to his essence, man is first of all an ek-sistence in and towards the "open-ness" of Being ("Offenheit", HB, 36). Man is then neither a subject within some subject-object relation that creates oppositions; nor is he a subject opening upon some unfolding History; nor is he searching for values to get hold of, thus objectifying them; nor is he any other of those consequences of a "subjectivity" that Heidegger critizes throughout the Letter as his negative leitmotiv (e.g., 8-9, 17, 20, 28, 35, 37, 43). This whole attempt at avoiding "subjectivity" is not only linked with reestablishing man in relation to Being, but it is also an effort to point to that domain out of which must arise a *fundamental ethic* (HB, 41) which is not only on this side, as it were, of the subject-object division but is also in a unity prior to the distinction of theory and praxis.

example [46a], does it follow that we have, even as a minimum basis, an authentic, essential, historical humanism? Not necessarily. One recognizes the logical fallacy of jumping to a positive conclusion, since other factors may account for the outcome. Furthermore, we know that the nature of this process is determined by the basic idea of *Entsprechen*; for, if the process falls within a merely existential structure, we have the problem of what contact it can really have with historical humanity. Supposing, however, that Heidegger's thought allows for a co-responding and not a mere correspondence of man and Being and that the process is linked to lived experience, there is still, in any case, another factor. Does Heidegger's undertaking, which goes through the overcoming-process come out in such a way that we may know — really, historically — where he, or we, are going? In other words, is there an effective communication? At the end, we shall indicate what may be the proper domain for asking such a question.

Before examining the class-B interpretation, we should compare the other two, for then the question will naturally arise: Is there some middle ground between such divergent interpretations? Would it be indicated by class-B?

In the C-interpretation, man's real place is to be the historical place of manifestation, the voice and instrument of Being; in A, this very notion is seen as necessarily depriving man of his human, creative activity and endangering his very existence. For the former, Being assures man of his dignity when he is in effective relationship to Being; for the latter, man loses his dignity, since there is no way for the relationship to take place as a humanizing act, and what comes to pass, if it does, is but the identification of man's dignity with the ineffable dignity of Being. The first group has no noetic worry nor do they wish to proclaim too much for man; the second are not satisfied with the "passivity" of the "waiting" rôle nor do they hold that man need, at least at this early stage, have recourse to the apophatic. The simple basic attitude of the C-interpreter is not appreciated by the others who see an inadmissible subordination of man such that he cannot really *read* the sense of history and of the manifestation of Being; consequently, to go along with Heidegger would be nothing more than to go forward by an act of the will or by some act of faith — unless one is already "there" in mystical poetry.

The contrast can be easily shown by one quotation from Müller [43]:

> Für Heidegger gibt es nur *ein* Thema des Philosophierens: Nicht den Menschen und die Existenz, sondern einzig und allein das Sein. Aber die Existenz und in ihr der Mensch ist Mittel und Ort und Grund der Möglichkeit und Ansatz für die Seinserhellung. (p. 17)

The question can be reduced to the one word "aber". For the C-interpreter, it signifies naturally "on the other hand"; the adversative force lies hidden in the ultimate mystery of the relationship of Being. The A-interpreter is stopped short: How can a "but" reconcile these two statements?[14]

CLASS-B

While being by in large less negatively critical than A, this group sharply focusses the problem of the Heideggerian approach. As concerns man, the event of Being is independent

---

[14] By taking only a couple of texts we can easily bring out further reasons for such a divergence.

Since Heidegger discovers at the center of the event a primacy of Being whose initiative he affirms, it is expected that he reaffirm this same prerogative for the event considered as the historical task and work which language constitutes :"Das Sein kommt, sich lichtend, zur Sprache" (HB, 45). He carefully adds, however, a rôle reserved to man: "So ist das Denken ein Tun" "...seinerseits in seinem Sagen zur Sprache... in die Lichtung des Seins gehoben". In a later work, *Unterwegs zur Sprache,* he will say that "Die Sprache *ist* Monolog", a striking but sticking formula. But this "monologue" *is* Being as described in the Letter, the same Being that comes "sich lichtend". Again the enigmatic formula of *Unterwegs* is tempered. For, as in the Letter, after saying that "the utterance is the way in which the event speaks" (i.e., that Being comes-to-pass [geschieht]), he carefully adds — again without indicating the intrinsic reason for "conciliating" the statements — that man is supposed to bring to this happening some sort of response (pp. 265-67).

of his will [22], man eventually becomes powerless in the face of Being [19] since there is not even a human referent to the Event [4a]; consequently, one does not find in man even an unrealizable existentiel exigency [42]. On the other hand, Being has been absolutized by being relegated to the realm of pure concepts [23] and to a pure, absolute zone [53]; it is unknowable [51] and inaccessible [48]. We have a subjectivistic type of thinking whose meta-humanism humanizes Being [35a]. If the subject is identified with the absolute, one arrives at a class-A interpretation with no properly human and personal action; if, however, a distinction is maintained, there is then the problem of what real relationship can be had between man and Being. Thus arises the question of how man can mediate [12, 22]. This question is put in various forms which, as a whole, seek more positively what is signified in Heidegger's thought as an indication of a possible way out of the difficulty because this problem can throw light on a perennial question. This way — or way out — is seen as an impersonal mystique [12], as a mysticism [28] or as a moving through "negative thought" to the positive aspect of the apophatic [19, 28]; or else, as a form of hope [17, and in effect, 23 and 28] and of the eschaton [23].

The problem stands quite intact, the question is what light may be thrown upon it. For we have authors who affirm a pure coming-to-pass of history without a real rôle for man and at the same time an eschatological position. What would be the basis of the latter within the former? Perhaps, again, it is only an unrealizable hope [17], which means that man's will-activity and faith are ungrounded; when recognized as such, this interpretation enters group-A.

As for the charge of idealism leveled at Heidegger by the members of group-B, no matter what their shading may be, they have this point in common: if the idealism is considered "innocuous", one remains within this group; if, however, one concentrates on the potential threat to man (and correlatively with some authors, the threat to the nature of the Absolute), then one passes over into the A-group.

Summarizing in terms of "subjectivistic idealism", one

would say that history, as an on-going-process without human referent, is irrelevant to real man, since it is essentially meta-historical, an unknowable conceptualization. In seeking, nevertheless, some real rapport, one must turn to some form of faith or mysticism; the former sometimes expressed as the eschatological, the latter as a humanly impersonal process, sc., a type of radical passivity — usually announced more palatably as radical "open-ness".

By means of the correlativity of the noetic (and, consequently, relevancy) let us compare the B-class interpretation with the others. Whereas noetic and epistemological shortcomings usually still open upon the possibility of man's historical mediating rôle, class-A finds merely a fruitless impasse, while C sees no difficulty due to the lived context, indeed to the "greater" context in which the problem is taken up — or merely "subsumed", as a good standing member of A-class would label it. The noetic question breaks down as follows: for B, there is perhaps the possibility of hope and of the eschatological; for A, there is merely a will-to-be (if not "power"); for C, there is an awareness of immediacy. This latter point, however, is viewed by A as the unwarranted assumption that *Entsprechen* means an act of truly responding, whereas B considers it as worthy of study in order to throw light on the possibility of true correspondence by examining what relevancy remains in the structured *Entsprechen* idea — at least we do consider this as an important expressed or unexpressed element of the more serious reflections in this area. Finally, all three groups recognize Heidegger's conception of man as an "instrument". This means for the C-members that man's rôle is to be the effective place of Being's manifestation; for A, man is reduced to an instrumental and hence dehumanized rôle. Again, we believe that many representatives of the B-class have the more nuanced position: while granting that man may be but some spectator before a process, the question is often put as to whether Heidegger has in fact failed to "overcome" metaphysics and, if so, whether he has fallen ironically into a Platonic position — in the rather cliché-sense of the term — namely, whether Being is so placed as to invite man to bridge two worlds. Thus, while many admit Heidegger's failure, they consider his treatment of the poet and of language as enlightening somewhat the revelatory process; consequently, this position finds a higher interest among theologians.

The allusion to theology brings us to an important consideration. What is there about Heidegger's thought, especially in the Letter as explicitated by later works, that permits such a range of conflicting interpretations? For theologians, the answer, or at least the principal and immediate reason is quite clear. Heidegger's expression is in part, but to a very important degree, a de-theologized language, as he himself admits; as a result, the theologian's content is absent and he is thereby encouraged to bring to the text his own "inspiration". Moreover, Heidegger's language is generally de-personalized; this fact allows many a philosopher the freedom to read into the text. Unfortunately, too many become unaware of the limitations of the text.

The radical divergence that we have personally witnessed in going through the literature surpasses by far any intrinsic reason that can be reasonably attributed to Heidegger's thought. The sad fact is that too many have written their first impressions without ever reading the text carefully; others have merely repeated the jargon of satellite thinkers, often worsened by a scant acquaintance with the text; others, finally, reading very selectively with their own ideas in mind, have grossly generalized. True, there is a small minority of very competent men but these should proceed more earnestly at de-mythologizing the literature, a process that this bibliography furthers when one considers attentively what the upshot of the data suggests. By in large, the interpretative process has gone awry and one should ask why. Indeed, this is one of Heidegger's indisputable lessons: to encourage one to be startled by the way things are going, e.g., man and technicity, man and the forgetfulness of Being, man and the course of history... the interpreter and the text!

We know that our philosopher has complained more than once that he has not been read carefully. In turning to page 36 of the Letter, we find an example of this justified complaint but we also have here the material for considering why, apart from what may be the reader's fault, there is, after all, abundant reason for divergent interpretations. Here we find two points: an example of "neutralizing" his thought such that one is invited to fill it out and a passage that even upon the most careful study becomes so enigmatic that it would seem most interpreters would have some basis for their view.

As for "neutralization", we discover that the proposition about man's essence as being-in-the-world does not decide the metaphysico-theological sense whether man is only a being in this world or of the other ("ein nur diesseitiges oder ob er ein jenseitiges Wesen sei"). Undoubtedly theologians find considerable liberty here, but then so does many a philosopher upon reading HB, 16: "Der Satz: 'Der Mensch ek-sistiert' antwortet nicht auf die Frage, ob der Mensch wirklich sei oder nicht, sondern antwortet auf die Frage nach dem 'Wesen' des Menschen" — the proposition: "man ek-sists" does not answer the question whether man is real or not, it answers the question concerning the "essence" of man. But he who considers seriously this proposition about a proposition knows that he cannot simply find the freedom he may think he had. What does the term "essence" — and in quotation marks at that — mean? If man is "nach dem Wesen", he is, for Heidegger, more real than "wirklich". "Wesen" does not have the meaning of "essence". Though we cannot here enter upon a discourse of Heidegger's thought, let us at least say that anyone who leaps at this proposition as being some proof of subjectivism or of "Platonism", or of some abstract world, is reading into the text. Yet, one of these categorizations may well be a valid interpretation of Heidegger's thought. But not because of *this* text.

Since we cannot within the purview of this little volume expound the difficulties of Heideggerian exegesis, which in their fundamental aspects are *one* with the central hermeneutical problem, we can, nevertheless, return to HB, 36 where, as we alluded (p. 70), the fundamental approach, that should be decisive for most serious interpretations, can be read in function of this crucial text: "Erst aus der Wahrheit des Seins...

Erst aus dem Wesen des Heiligen... Erst im Lichte... nennen soll". This text reveals where Heidegger is going and for "Heideggerians" — and perhaps not exclusively — where philosophical thought is heading.

We can only outline in a questioning fashion what may come to mind for many a well-informed and well-intentioned reader of Heidegger. This passage spells out a general approach indicative of Heidegger's overall intention which has motivated his work. But is this outline meant to be merely one of method? — that is, a general method in which one proceeds patiently and in order, going from one stage to another, from a clarified ground to another to be opened up? Or does this approach affirm some real philosophical content such that it is a program to be carried out by historical, explicative interpretation? Or, finally, is it prophetic? — that is, less of a philosophical endeavor than a pointing to the nature ("Wesen and "Anwesen") of the coming-Event of Being? Whatever may be the content of Heidegger's intention, the question remains as to whether it can be carried out within his framework. If one answers the last question with a most dubious yes, as well he might, one should be inclined to consider this entire approach as some expression of hope; if one answers with a clear negative, then, this hope becomes some courageous act of (philosophical?) faith. In a word, is Heidegger's approach fundamentally optimistic as to its realization? Finally, apart from Heidegger's framework, or even inspite of it, as the case may be, is this approach valid?

This line of questioning puts into focus the standard problem of whether there is any existentiel content to his thought and, if there is, whether it is compatible with his notion of *Entsprechen* and the rest of his thought.

Our passage under consideration draws out, moreover, most of the other central points of contention. Is the approach an expression of the eschatological? Some would say that the statement is merely a device to put off indefinitely questions that Heidegger does not wish to handel, or cannot, or even dare not face. On the contrary, it may not be merely eschatological but a grounded philosophical view that the advent of language and of Being's language (in order to reveal Being) is already *underway*. In such a case, we have the problem of whether man with passive "attention" merely waits for the language to come and to speak to (or even *in*) him; or, to state it more simply, whether there is room for true human activity to bring this about. If, of course, we have absolutized Being into a deterministic shadow, then man's action is nothing — nothing but, perhaps, than the hastening of that which will come anyhow. But, if no such shadow is had and man does have a creative rôle to play, we have the ground for an authentic humanism for the stark reason that in this context there can be no other ground. On the other hand, the student of Heidegger recalls that since we are still in the epochal time of decadent metaphysics, humanism and technicity, then how in the world can we — or more precisely, Heidegger — ever see enough *now* to ground such an approach, including its hope and its ability to recognize what in fact would be the "overcoming" of the present situation. Certainly, it is difficult to appeal to better thinking times, as an urgent call to a fidelity to Being's history by returning now through a "recapturing" (Wiederholung) of the lost purity of pre-Socratic thought. For what real knowledge do we have of that ? Would we know *historisch* — not to mention *geschichtlich* — the distinction from some "sub-Socratic thought" ?

Perhaps Pöggeler is right, there is no content to Heidegger's approach. We are offered a *way*, at least indirectly in helping us to bring out the meaning and significance of experience. But, then, Pöggeler has never really brought into question the fundamental basis of Heidegger's endeavor; specifically, whether such a "way" is radically capable of being lived in order to be known. It must contain a content of experience, otherwise it is difficult to see how it could even be communicated. And the communicability of Heidegger's thought is not the least of problems.

Our questions centered about the crucial text of the Letter (p. 36) can be summarized as follows. Is there reason to know or believe, or even hope, that the *Ankommendes* is either at hand or is already acting ? Or is the author merely restating the "revealing-revealed" and "hiding-hidden" nature of events, perhaps to the point of stating it as the sum of the possibilities of some future Coming. But through a concern centered on the Advent of Being, it would seem that we have left the question of man behind. Not at all. The questioning is perfectly correlative. Is man's attitude *ontologically* restricted to some wishful thinking or does it become meaningful and responsible behavior? Can he act *with* Being? Or is his "authentic" thinking-activity merely that of Being's? — if so, he would be but a quasi-phenomenological being, some living-bracket to be fulfilled by the advent of Language — if it comes. On the contrary, one would want to account for a creative "awaiting" such that man is involved by and through his fundamental *ethos* and realizes himself according to his *essence*. With its verbal force, "essence" means the timely-historical thrust of (self-) realization; consequently, man, as an individual, would be *called* upon to realize himself. Here one recognizes the basis for an authentic humanism.

But we cannot say that the foregoing is Heidegger. More important, we cannot say that it is not. Why?

We know that a divergence of interpretations is encouraged by the "neutral" language, especially with reference to the existentiel and the onto-theo-logical. But along these lines, it does not matter that much which interpretation is held. For the questioning does not come to grips at the basic level of an encounter with Heidegger's thought.

The more positive reason for the divergence as well as for the fact that most questions put to Heidegger are at least somewhat tangential is the relative neglect of the myth element in his thought. A searching consideration for the élan of our questioning elicited by our chosen passage must reveal, at the price of non-sense, the myth factor, or if one prefers, the symbolic. Then, and only then, need we not face the facile choice of one interpretation over against another. The issue lies at a deeper level of interpretation.

We must note, however, that class-B has the highest percentage of interpreters explicitly aware of the symbolic element in play. It is for this reason, we believe, that the extreme positions tend not to appear; namely, one does not find literal or "naïve" interpretations of the words of the text that favor an existentialistic position (as many C-interpreters do) nor does one find a simplistic, logical extrapolation of the negative factor (as do too many in group-A) because the context is better upheld through a recognition of the symbolic and apophatic dimensions of thought.

Our examination of Heideggerian literature implies in large part its demythologization, or more exactly, its urgent need thereof; in a stricter sense, it is Heidegger himself who must be demythologized — and considerably so. But one cannot go the whole way, nor should one. It is especially clear since the Letter that he has demythologized man and Being, and philosophy and theology, to come up again with myth — a myth that may well be used to better think through our times. Reality is such that we may not proceed and live without myth. History and revelation are such that we may not conceive it, communicate or signify it without the symbolic as an essential and signifying element.

Heidegger's message, *nolens volens,* is that the "way" contains myth and myth cannot be read or effectively communicated in the third person. There is no question of being "faithful" to his thought but only whether his thought may help one to be closer to a faithful response to the exigences of the real, that is, *geschichtlich* and *eigentlich* thinking. The question is whether one dare expose himself to serious questioning and reflecting; only then, does it become clear that any attempt to evaluate our philosopher's thought *as such* is, to say the least, no longer a relevant question.

IV

CRITICAL BIBLIOGRAPHY

LIST OF SYMBOLS:

Authors-

    A — refers always to the particular author in question
    H — refers always to Heidegger

Classifications of interpretations-

    A — anti-humanism
    B — meta-humanism
    C — authentic humanism
    D — unclassified
            For detailed classification, cf. pp. 65-66.

Works of Heidegger-

    EM : *Einführung in die Metaphysik*
    FW : *Der Feldweg*
    HB : *Über den Humanismus* [*Humanismusbrief*]
    HW : *Holzwege*
    ID : *Identität und Differenz*
    KM : *Kant und das Problem der Metaphysik*
    PW : *Platons Lehre von der Wahrheit. Mit einem Brief über den "Humanismus"*
    SG : *Der Satz vom Grund*
    SZ : *Sein und Zeit*
    US : *Unterwegs zur Sprache*
    WD : *Was heisst Denken?*
    WG : *Vom Wesen des Grundes*
    WM : *Was ist Metaphysik?*
    WW : *Vom Wesen der Wahrheit*

PAGINATION:

All pagination within parentheses refers to the particular work in question.

All pagination within square brackets refers to the text of the Letter, either as HB, 5-47 (for the separate printing) or as PW, 53-119 (for the text printed with *Platons Lehre von der Wahrheit*) — cf. note, p. 23. One will note that no confusion is possible since the two series are mutually exclusive.

A correlation of HB and PW will be found at the end.

1. [C]   ACHARD-ABELL, Marcelle. "Heidegger et la poésie de Saint-John Perse. Un rapprochement". *Revue de métaphysique et de morale*, 71(1966), 292-306.

Humanism, though not formally treated, is clearly implied even apart from the ten references to HB. The poet's breaking through the world of constructs is read in terms of H's own justification against attacks of illogism and irrationalism [HB, 34]. The A's comparison, however, leads somewhat too facilely to the poet as the ideal, and to H's thought as an exemplification, of a truly lived effort "to be man" — "to be man is to speak". This straight existentiel interpretation implies authentic humanism. Though perhaps one should not expect to find in this type of article a treatment of any difficulties peculiar to Heideggerian interpretation; still, it is strange that it does not consider the meaning of the theme taken from Hölderlin: "man dwells poetically...". Certainly it is central to this article and, as we know, it is of the very crux of the question of "humanism" precisely in the sense of what it means "to be man".

2. [A]   ALCORTA, José Ignacio. "El humanismo de Heidegger". *Sapientia* (La Plata), 15 (1960), 7-17, 107-119.

"Homo humanus" implies the problem of humanism since the humanization of man is possible only by uncovering the true being of his essence. "Humanism" sometimes means the obvious and generalized sense of its historical interpretations; other times, it aims at interpreting Being and the essence of man. It betrays a dialectical juxtaposition of realism and idealism. Supposing that out of fundamental thinking of Being, one does reach an adequate notion of man, the problem for H remains: the reality of *man* as *being*. The question is more than theoretical, it is practical and normative. Yet, there is in H some distinction between determining the notion of humanism and its realization. Ek-sistence is not somebody else's expression but is of someone who is in the possible modes of existence which, though neither psychological nor moral, represent a decision, even on the theoretical plane.

This study should draw respect in the way it poses and preserves the question. Though for example (cf. no. 9a, p. 80) some state the ambiguity that "Dasein is both the being of man and the truth of Being", they often proceed to eliminate it. The A follows through: if one can discover the essence of man, would it be man's?

3. [D] ALLEMANN, Beda. *Hölderlin und Heidegger*. 2. Aufl. Atlantis Verlag, Zürich und Freiburg i.B., 1956. 224 pp.

The A's exposition of Hölderlin is followed (60-71) immediately by that of the *Kehre* [esp. HB, 17] with the evident significance that it is a turning to a new language after the failure of the "metaphysical" to be able to think the ontological difference — and that this is in effect the new way, or as Pöggeler will say, the Second Way (cf. no. 46a, p. 215f). Thus, the A refutes this "turning" as being from the existential to Being (sc., as found in nos. 10 and 37). Humanism (164) is treated in the expected context of HB, 11 which characterizes Hölderlin as thinking more originatively the destiny (Geschick) of man's essence; consequently, one must examine the meaning of "*Natur*". But here (as in 101ff) it is hard to know the nature of the dialogue and of the distance ("Kluft") between poetizing and thinking. Though the A takes up various aspects of the problem (e.g., H's language, 111ff), there is no attempt to arrive at an overall, or even penetrating, interpretation of H — which is probably best, given the narrow basis of Hölderlin as the one source of inspiration.

The value of this competent book on Hölderlin is, for our purpose, the underlining of the fact that this poet is a key to understanding why H turns (kehrt) to the question of humanism in the way he does but it leaves open all the essential questions, since it is unclear in what sense he understands and accepts the poet and esp. the key notion of *Heimkehr* (136) transposed precisely into the domain of a new "humanism" in terms of a turning back to Being.

4a. [B] ASTRADA, Carlos. "Fondamenti ontologici esistenziali dell'umanesimo". *Rivista di filosofia*, 43 (1952), 372-86.

Almost the entire article is in function of H and esp. HB which is seen as a meta-humanism ("sopra-humano"). An a-historical myth (380) in terms of Being becomes ever more mythologized and is finally absolutized without man's historical referent ("attribuzione di senso da parte del Dasein a una istanza sopra-temporale"). After accepting too uncritically H's historical analysis of humanism (374-5), the A attempts to point to a way out; it is too late except for some form of eclecticism. The absence of a serious consideration of language is surprising, though the A could not turn to US (posterior to this study) for an abundance of ammunition. The suggested analysis of where H is going seems by in large defensible. It would have been better to develop it rather than outline how the A would re-establish his own position.

4b. "Über die Möglichkeit einer existenzial-geschichtlichen Praxis". In: *Martin Heideggers Einfluss auf die Wissenschaften* (verfasst von ASTRADA, BAUCH, et. al.), A. Francke AG Verlag, Bern, 1949, pp. 165-71.

A rather disappointing study, perhaps in part explanable by its early date. Though tangential to the HB question, it is tightly related by the interpretation of the internal continuity and of the concrete problematic of H's thought. The A summarizes the possibility of an existential-historical praxis according to SZ ("Wiederholung", "Geschick" and Dasein as Existenz) — without new clarification — and stresses fundamental action (Handeln) as distinct, according to its originality, from the practical and theoretical (Verhalten); yet, he never alludes to the parallel development in HB [45-6] but deems it proper to cite HB only as a parting appeal for a "productive dialogue with Marxism". Furtheremore, he overstates his case: "die Praxis die Theorie bestimmt, und nicht die Theorie die Praxis, wie *alle* bisherige Philosophie annahm" — we underline the neglect, to say the least, of Marx and Blondel.

5. [D]   AXELOS, Kostas. *Einführung in ein künftiges Denken. Über Marx und Heidegger.* Max Niemeyer Verlag, Tübingen, 1966. 104 pp.

A collection of lectures of which only the first, "Marx and Heidegger. Wegweiser eines Denkens", is pertinent. The first two pages, except for a couple of connectives, are taken from HB's treatment of Marx and of *téchnê*. With this setting, it is expected that the explication of our question (36ff) brings out two points: alienation and the real possibility of becoming man. HB is seen as calling for "the overcoming of the naturalistic-psychological-sociological-humanistic interpretation of man through a thinking that dares to ask in what way the essence of man belongs to the truth of Being". The man of humanism is one of "home-lessness, alienation, subjectivism and objectivism", he is rendered incapable of reflection and of daring to ask the question. The A relates this position to that of "early" Marx. Though often too uncritical, this study lacks no imagination; some of the pertinent texts of HB stand out with a new poignancy from their Marxist counterpart. It is *only* the formation of such a context that, for our purpose, is of interest.

6. [A]   AZEVEDO, Juan Llambias de. "Der alte und der neue Heidegger". *Philosophisches Jahrbuch,* 60 (1950), 161-74.

SZ is de-theologized philosophy with a Kantian twist: a rationalist subjectivism becomes the irrationalist fondamental structure of the being of Dasein, this is a transcendental anthropology *or* humanism. This approach is then (esp. in HB) simply set aside and left unresolved; H's philosophy is no longer either critical or anthropological or nihilistic. Furthermore it is unkown where H is going: poetry, or religion, or some completely new expression of the spirit (Geist). The A's interpretation falls into the "unclassified" but the unresolved intrinsic reasoning adduced favors class-A. His analysis, however, imposes unwarranted theological categories even though there can be a partial justification for such development, just as there is for the very interesting set of quotations from HB where he proposes that "God" or "Logos" be read instead of "Being" (171) in order to bring out the characteristics of H's concept. His insistence that H once espoused a secularized fall of man should at least have considered the formal protest of HB, 21.

7 [A]   BATTAGLIA, Felice. *Heidegger e la filosofia dei valori.* Il Mulino, Bolognia, 1967.

The A is a most clear representative of class-A: "man" and "ethics" are respectively emptied of sense. There is a structural identity of the ontic and the ontological into one of the All-embracing ("Uno-tutto"); as a necessary consequence, the requirements of man's presence to Being become exactly those of God's in order to be in the immediate, effective presence of man. In such a framework, the ethical can have no sense, axiology is an impossibility. While appreciating H's critique of value-philosophy, the A claims that it has assimilated everything and, with the concomitant requisites of Being, the "transient fate of man is of no importance": he is de-humanized (91). Cf. esp. 28-37, 81-88.

This most pointed critique is well reasoned; the A attempts honestly to explain the question through H. Of particular interest is the faithful summary of H's intention in condemning "values": he exposes H's idea of value, especially through SZ, EM and HW, such as to set up the scene for the appearance of HB and, then, for an understanding of what he considers to be the excesses of H.

8. [C]   BEAU, Albin Eduard. "O Humanismo no pensamento de Heidegger". *Humanitas* (Coimbra), 2 (1949), 195-210.

Through a positive and well balanced summary exposition stressing the unity and continuity of PW-HB, the A underlines H's defence against the charges of anti-humanism, irrationalism, positivism, atheism and nihilism, while developing briefly the logic of his thinking "against values". H's intention comes through clearly and is proposed as a voice to which one should listen in today's confused discussion of humanism, characterized as "a mental crisis of the age". This voice has a real and significant contribution to make. The article encourages the reader's assent but warns of "the danger inherent in the radicalism" of H's critique.

Our classification C must be highly qualified for it is not so much a question of H's own thought leading to an authentic humanism as H being a stimulus that should encourage rigorous examination of conscience and re-examination of traditional concepts as a basis for restoring a sense to humanism.

9a. [C]   BIRAULT, Henri. "Existence et vérité d'après Heidegger". *Revue de métaphysique et de morale*, 56 (1951), 35-87. [Also in: Phénoménologie-Existence. Recueil d'études par BIRAULT, VAN BREDA *et al.* A. Collin, Paris, 1953, pp. 139-191].

This is an illuminating attempt at unraveling the relational knot of truth, ek-sistence and liberty in view of the hidden ground of the essence of man in order to express the framework for an overcoming of "humanism", especially as a Cartesian relic responsable for both Christian and atheistic humanism; in the process the A tries to point out an authentic way inspired by what is the "living unity of Heideggerian thought". The "engagement" of HB is compared to the *Entschlossenheit* of SZ, even while stressing Being as donor and gift. Between thought and faith an abyss exists, thus the central question becomes: how is thought "saving". One must get beyond the word "humanism" since the process of overcoming metaphysics and humanism is one.

The interpretation (83-6) of HB's humanism suggests a profound link with the destruction of the sacred or holy. But this becomes enmeshed in a pure eschatological form, perhaps due to the fact that the A mentions the poet and the sacred while saying nothing about his naming the sacred. Furthermore, there is some confusion between structural and historical thought (cf. pp. 64-5 "Verhältnis, Verhalten"; p. 80, the unannounced transition from Dasein to Man and from Man to man) even though the A has well criticized the taking of Dasein as "human reality".

9b.   "De l'être, du divin et des dieux chez Heidegger". In: *L'existence de Dieu* (Cahiers de l'actualité religieuse, 16), Casterman, Tournai, 1961, pp. 49-76.

This study explicitates a point implied above: the destruction of metaphysics is bound up with the process of de-divinization. The latter development is clearly and sympathetically outlined, and related to H's attack on humanism [theo-metaphysical]. Though de-divinization and anti-humanism (in its determined, rejected sense) are effectively linked, there is unfortunately no development of the theme. The question of humanism is seen as "solidaire" with H's larger perspective of a critique going beyond the metaphysical suppositions of Nietzsche.

10. [A]   Bollnow, Otto Friedrich. "Heideggers neue Kehre". *Zeitschrift für Religions- und Geistesgeschichte*, 2 (1949/50), 113-128.

One finds an exposition of HB in terms of the "turning", indeed, of a radical reversal ("eine radikale Umkehr") that provides two basic readings carefully argued from the text: first (to p. 120) a clear reading of what the text means and where it is going logically; then, through probing questioning an interpretation of its basic meaning. In this part the A leaves us in the air with H, not without irony and deduces that H's humanism — though not according to his intention — would be impossible for the A. The "new" approach is likened to form and content, one in which man would be a mere instrumental mouthpiece ("Sprachrohr") of Being who does the acting, the thinking; the speaking for "Seinsverständnis" of Dasein has become Being's act. Thus man is so rooted in Being that he is lost. The A's reasoning concerning the notions of *Überwindung* and of the medium of encounter is particularly forceful and should be considered seriously in any evaluation of our problematic. Of the A's two books and six articles studied as pertaining to our subject, this is surely the most incisive. The new approach of the "Kehre-humanism" becomes, in effect, an *Ent-humansierung* of man — which is more serious than implying an anti-position.

11. [C] Braido, Pietro. "L'umanesimo 'ontologico' di M. Heidegger contro l'umanesimo 'esistenzialistico' di J.-P. Sartre". *Salesianum* (Torino), 14 (1952), 1-25.

Through a contrast with Sartre, the A wishes to dispel ambiguities and bring out H's "anti-'humanistic'humanism". In giving back a sense to the word "humanism", Being, should be the norm of the word; true humanism must be reconquered by turning back to man and starting with Being itself — such is the "exclusively essential" step of "all genuine humanism" (16). But we then read mere paraphrasing of H punctuated with "assurances" (e.g., "Hinaustehen" assures the dignity of man, in this "il più serio e solido umanesimo"); then follow carefully selected, balanced phrases without the shadow of a problem. The only reserve is that H has insisted almost exclusively on the "destructive part" — unaware perhaps that the positive is to arise out of the same process.

Man has a way or a call that awaits the accomplishment

of its "ontological" part. Though this word is now most suspect with H, the A invokes it as the key to this sudy and insists that authenic humanism will be formulated in its concrete structure when this ontology will be realized (21). This is the way. But then the A has more faith than most. The parts do not fit too well; indeed, the concluding observations (23-5) should be dropped because they are made from the remotest clime of Heideggerian thought such that H is either the complete philosophy-of-life man, a critical realist, a Thomist, or *Sein* knows what, if it knows.

12. [B]   BREEK, B. "Heidegger en de ethiek". *Nederlands theologisch Tijdschrift,* 13 (1958/9), 190-205.

In proposing a fundamentally new ethos, rather than an ethic, H overcomes the duality of Being and "Gehören" (hearing, attending, obeying) through the concrete originality of building-dwelling-thinking whose theory-praxis, bound up with art and the poetic expressions, requires one to think about the path which is already one of service to Being. But in this process, as marked esp. by HB, 38, the personal factor to mediate the call of Being becomes lost, later (in ID) the needed relationship is simply posited as the fact of man as relation (Bezug). By an *inner* necessity, the more H works out his doctrine of Being, the more he gets entangled in this problem. For the A, this suggests, especially through the notion of the "jump" or "leap" (explicitated in SG), that there is no fundament other than Christ. He proposes St. Paul in place of the *Lichtung* of some impersonal mystique of Being ("zijns-mystiek"). Such is the impasse of H — which seems to us as not too subtle a fashion to say that H's thought cannot withstand the bracketing of the personal nature of service to, and the call of, Being.

The A's reasoning commands respect. However, one would expect: some explicitation of H's failure to carry out the idea of "Mitsein" (as well as of love which is touched upon without an intrinsic link up); some recognition of the rôle of symbolism (the "Geviert" is mentioned without recognizing the different planes involved); some connection of the critique of

"Bezug" with the opening page of HB; some better selection of points (which are too diffused) to bring out more carefully the A's stages of development (the A moves too quickly, even dating a passage from HB as if it were from PW proper); finally, his method is unclear. Does he employ some Jaspersian reading of a "cipher of failure"? What is the exact connection between the two parts of the article? Nevertheless, this outline should call for serious consideration no matter what one may think of the author's own leap at the end. It is most central to our question.

13. [A]   BRUNNER, August. "Umschau: Holzwege". *Stimmen der Zeit*, 146 (1949/50), 226-9.

Though this article is intended as a study of HW, we have in fact a remarkably compact critique of a main point of HB: man as the place of Being and the possibility of a personal rôle in his function as the "house of Being". The A judges that man appears only as the place (Stätte) of revelation with a consequent de-personalization of man which, through Dilthey, has been mesmerized by the "Abgrund des Lebens". This explains the crucial text, "Das Sein hat den Menschen als ek-sistierenden... selbst ereignet" [94]: a non-personal ("unpersönlich") subject with no creative ground out of which could arise a person through the interplay of the hiding-revealing activity of Being.

This critique clearly implies the impossibility of any humanizing action with a logic that is quite formidable; its argument, however, moves too closely in the shadow of one narrow interpretation of SZ, granted that, at the time of writing, H's auto-interpretations had not yet made their impact.

14. [C]   BUDDEBERG, Else. *Denken und Dichten des Seins. Heidegger, Rilke*. Metzler, Stuttgart, 1956. 210 pp.

The theme of humanism is not professedly treated, yet, in reading HB in terms of Rilke a definite interpretation is unavoidable: it implies our class-C, within, if this is possible, class-

B. For HB is characterized as a personal expression ("diction menschlich-persönlich") while its content is interpreted structurally with startling clarity (e.g., Being-over-all and There-being and vice versa). The poet is the very form of the Letter's "engagement" and since man is the shepherd of Being, we should look to this Letter with the poet. Unfortunately, HB has no such clarity and its style is hardly to be recommended as personal.

15. [C]   CASALONE, Pietro. "La filosofia ultima di Heidegger". *Rivista di filosofia neo-scolastica* (Milano), 50 (1958), 117-137.

Though HB is referred to only five times without thematizing our question, the classification of a real and pure authenticity implying a "new path" of humanism is evident. Man's task is "to put himself anew to the revelation of Being and to feel himself called to name things" (136) through experiencing the original hope of Being by which he feels thrown into Being with the responsibility of conserving and assuring its revelation in language. H has come down to the world to confound all his critics (117-8) through a long and difficult "iter philosophicum"; his way, the A assures us, has the mysterious calling of a church bell. There are two moments: an ascendency and a descent, the "momento esistenziale" problematizing the "human condition" analogously to Pascal and Kierkegaard, and the "momento decisamente ontologico" which is Being's that resolves and absolves the prior.

The A's poetic, if not naïve, clearness is perhaps explained by his recent reading of FW. How else explain the fact that he speaks on one page (119) of destiny, epochal history, H as the prophet of Being, error, transcendency and Nothingness with no shadow at all of any problematic? In good Heideggerianese: the vision's clarity con-fuses man, existence and Being. It is an open question whether H is, or should be proposed as, everybody's prophet. Apparently, the A's enthusiasm has beclouded this fact.

16. [D]   CASTANOS DE MÉDICIS, Stélos. *Réponse à Heidegger sur l'humanisme*. A. Padrone, Paris, 1966. 92 pp.

Judging from its title, one would expect this book to bear most directly on our subject; unfortunately, it does not at all. It is a personal reflection that never comes to grips with H's question nor even his elementary thought. Interpretations of HB are hermetical, with no evidence of knowledge of other works to aid its hermeneutic intent. Basically a plea for "la philosophie vitale", it ends with an encomium of truth (86). H's historical question on "humanism" is a mere *lis de verbis* (36). The A purports to touch the essence of H (33-4); perhaps he does, but it is quite beyond us, as is this essential point: "Le faire exister l'être ou faire que l'existant soit être, où, mieux, les dimensions possibles où se font, où s'accordent l'un et l'autre, est le problème essentiel de toute philosophie" (60). One is led to suspect that the use of H in the title is to draw attention to this book which, perhaps, could have had in its own right some philosophical interest.

17a. [B]   CHIODI, Pietro. *L'ultimo Heidegger. 2a edizione*. Taylor, Torino, 1960. 138 pp.

An exceptionally clear, concise and competent study done by the Italian translator of *SZ, SG* and *HW*. The exposition is midly critical of H's intention; it shows his anti-humanism as identical to an anti-metaphysical and anthropological nihilism, etc. The critical section is relatively long and examines H's thought according to "undeniable" existentialistic exigences: it is a decapitated Hegelianism which by putting the "resolution" back into the history of Being in relation to man, reduces, *geschichtlich*, man to an instrument.

The critical section is in part over-logical and marred by a somewhat scholastic imposition (e.g., against Luther). It stangely lacks the clarity of the exposition, which should be noted for the historical linking up of the question of HB in PW (33-37), the restatement according to the Letter [81-105 with 51-53], and the driving motive ("motivo conduttore") related with other works (16). Because of the balanced exposition, the A belongs to a highly qualified B-class: man is an instrument (105) of a necessary structure (passim) of a neo-Platonic type (102) whose de-humanization (110) is tempered with a romantic hope of a way which is, however, unrealizable (111).

17b. "Heidegger e la fine della ragione astuta". *Rivista di filosofia* (Torino), 51 (1960), 398-425.

This article is part of the second edition of the book above.

18. [C] COLLINS, James. *The Existentialists. A Critical Study.* A Gateway-edition. Henry Regnery Company, Chicago, 1952.

This rich, analytical and synthetical critique done in function of the whole tradition of Western philosophy is very sympathetic to H. The A stresses the themes of the non-anthropocentric view, homelessness and, consequently, homecoming as a "closeness to the truth of being" which, as a return to origins, is the essential thinking as found in HB, 54-56, 111. Such thought is "the initial act which supplies the basis for all particular [and ethical] actions" (192) and in the context of "participation in being" allows man "to become truly human" (202). Only in this sense H acknowledges his thought as a humanism which is at the presuppositionless beginning prior to the distinction theory-praxis. H represents an "ontologized ethics" rather than an ontology at the expense of ethics.

We imagine a lack of space prevents the A from justifying a notion of participation, an attempt undertaken by Müller (no. 43, pp. 219-49); still, he should have mentioned the difficulty as well as the danger of reading a Thomistic attitude. Finally, he places with excessive emphasis (171-3) HB into an apologetic framework.

19. [B] COLUMBO, Arrigo. *Martin Heidegger. Il ritorno dell' essere.* Il Mulino, Bologna, 1964. 726 pp.

This work is somewhat the Italian counterpart of Richardson's (no. 47a). Its carefully detailed scholarship neatly separates exposition from conscious interpretation. Since the vast range of the book is ordered in terms of the problematic of contemporary society and its way of thinking — against which HB reacts — its interpretation of humanism takes on special values, esp. pp. 452-505 (in particular, 503f) where HB is linked in and out of H's works and pp. 631-2 which make a very pointed reduction to an impasse characterizing HB. H's "humanism" is a work against alienation (626) but man becomes absolutely powerless in front of Being (637). Only some "indices" (634) and the esthetic (674) remain as momentary clearings that cannot dissipate the fog from the way. The A ends with his own treatment of the apophatic which had some preparation in a prior reading of a negative theology and ontology in H.

One must admit, however, that the A has too many long digressions (e.g., Aquinas, Augustine) leading to unwarranted diffusiveness. He falls under a class-B interpretation but not as clearly as may first appear because in going through the very impasse of Dasein to the continued search of man, etc., he takes H prophetically. The method, in particular the nexus between such an exposition and its interpretation, should have been explicitated. Personally we find an apophatic sign, a "cipher"; if this be not the case, it becomes frightfully unclear what the A means by H, the Prophet.

20a. [C] DONDEYNE, Albert. "La différence ontologique chez Martin Heidegger". *Revue philosophique de Louvain*, 56 (1958), 35-62; 251-93.

Though the main theme of this study is Being, the correlative one of man implies the entire HB. The question of Being becomes the searching in ourselves for what makes encounter possible, it concerns the human meaning ("sens") of the experience of the "Es gibt" (62) [82]. Thus, " 'Sorge' signifying 'responsibility for', 'openness to the call of' makes one spontaneously think of the Marcellian idea of fidelity" (282).

Real dialogue (call, response, encounter, responsibility), communication, participation and open-ended transcendence are assumed throughout. If this interpretation is legitimate, one would like to see some questions — e.g., whether H deals merely with the possibility of the possibility (263) —; instead, one finds himself moving in and out of H's thought accompanied by Thomas and Marcel with the fear that too much is brought *to* this thought. One is quite free to suggest Gabriel Marcel but this cannot be a substitute for a grounding attempt of H's "existentiel" thought. We find H moving, without fear of the opposite, on the existentiel plane. This study still remains as such a remarkable bit of research, esp. if one recognizes its suppositions.

20b. *Foi chrétienne et pensée contemporaine.* 2e ed. Publications universitaires de Louvain. Paris-Louvain. 1952. 211 pp.

This work does not modify our above critique. Once again one reads a Thomistic intuition of an "existentiel" approach and, still more clearly (48-9), one finds no account of the ground for a transition. There are simply no reasons at all adduced to justify putting Marcel, and specifically his notion of hope, into the *same* framework as HB.

21. [A] DUFRENNE, Mikel. *Pour l'homme.* Collection "Esprit". Editions du Seuil, Paris, 1968.

This book is a strong plea for a real and historical man against the influence of H's anti-humanism upon the basic tendency of French Structuralism moving towards the death of man after that of God. H's idea of history is the historical of Being, of Logos and the universe of discourse in which man is inserted ("structuralism") and where he becomes an instrument of impersonal thought and anonymous language ("positivism"). Cf. esp. chapter 1 and pp. 102, 117f, 165f, 183.

The nature of this work precludes any detailed argumentation on H; its interest lies in the nexus between H and the French structuralistic and positivistic tendencies of contemporary thought. In this, it is undoubtedly thought provoking and should encourage reflection on a fairly neglected point. One would have wished, however, that the A had cited a more readily available edition of H in the first chapter.

22. [B] FINAZZO, Giancarlo. *L'Uomo e il mondo nella filosofia di M. Heidegger.* Editrice Studium, Roma, 1963. 164 pp.

In this book on man, reality and Being, the HB-question finds its natural place. The A concludes (154) that the problematic of the function of Dasein, guardian of Being, constitutes one of the most complex points of H's thought; its mediating rôle assigned to man is intended to pressage a new humanism but its analysis does not shed light on Being so that man appears deprived of an absolute. For man's being is without finality such that there is but a pure coming-to-pass explained (28ff) as a pre-human finality, an apophatic; revelation of Being is a phenomenon outside man ("extra-umano"), independent of his will activity. In this context is explained the thinking of Being as a structural phenomenon of man [42].

This line of argumentation is very well reasoned but must be disengaged carefully since the A interposes scholastic categories. Had he considered H's thought on man as relation, he could then have asked legitimately whether man is without a relation to the absolute. Furthermore, the A makes the hasty charge of atheism and neglects the important distincion between will and liberty. Without keeping in mind H's idea of liberty, one cannot go too far, we believe, in evaluating his thought on the possibility of human action.

23. [B] FRIEDMANN, Georges. "Heidegger et la crise contemporaine de l'idée de progrès". *Cahiers internationaux de sociologie* (Paris), 16 (1954), 118-25.

The A leans heavily upon followers of H in order to reach (presumably more quickly) the basic point of his critique: H is himself in the shadow of that very "individualism" for which he had so roundly condemned Descartes; in order to give back man's dignity, his thought appeals to a Nostalgic Return and the possible coming of God; while claiming to think man more originally, he brackets the real situation. Not only do we do not know the nature of that "Golden Age" which seems to have preceded Heideggerian wisdom by some three millennia, but the discussion on humanism "does not go beyond the universe of pure concepts".

H's thought, therefore, has nothing to do with the real world of man. The article's brevity makes a critique difficult. It is certainly accurate in giving the thrust of some key disciples and quite acceptable when one recalls how little H is explicit on the sociological dimension. Still, one would have expected to read at least a word on what sociological possibilities, if any, are had in the notion of *Mitsein* and in particular, what, if any, of this idea is left in the later H of HB.

24. [D]   FÜRSTENAU, Peter. *Heidegger, das Gefüge seines Denkens.* "Philosophische Abhandlungen", 16. Bd. Klostermann, Frankfurt/M., 1958. 185 pp.

This is more of a survey than an overall view of H's thought structure. Our classification is D because this book is by in large a series of quotations whose nexi are due more to insight, or mere association of ideas, than to a reasoned theme; consequently, it is extremely difficult reading. HB is treated 73-100 (esp. 73-9) in a framework that is quite baffling. Given the author's theme, that it is high-time for an explicitation of structure as the first step for Heideggerian discussion (in which other authors are brushed brazenly aside, p. 3), and given the fact that there is a lack of sincere discussion on whether such a structure is to be found and whether H would be particularly pleased if one did discover or fabricate one, the "development" arrives at an unusual emphasis upon man in HB, all while speaking of "work" in structural terms as being that of Being's (79). HB is interpreted by stressing the ideas of "Macht" and "Geschick" both as an unfolding (Entfaltung) of Being, such that, frankly, the reader is left wondering what meaning human action could have in Heidegger or in any one else's thought.

25. [A]   GENT, Werner. "Existenzphilosophie und Ethik". *Philosophische Studien* (Berlin), 2 (1950), 126-36.

This compact article represents a pure, limit-case of the A-class and has historical and psychological interest in that the body was written before the A had read HB. H is taken as the forerunner and representative of "Existenzphilosophie", his philosophy is one of man, a mystical anthropology, his ethics is nihilistic, pessimistic and heroic — a blend somehow more firm because of H's twice stated Jesuit connections. In the epilogue added upon reading HB, the A finds complete confirmation and stresses two prior points: Atheism and the relation between ontology and ethics — yet, both of these points are left up in the air, as he closes each with the expression: "Jedenfalls...". He then reiterates H's "atheism" and religious "indifferentism" [HB, 36 !]. An author is free to ignore the Kehre, the question of Being, H's auto-interpretations and formal denials of many of these categories; still, to be honest, he should show his awareness of texts apparently stating the opposite.

26. [A] GERBER, Rudolph J. "Heidegger: Thinking and Thanking Being". *The Modern Schoolman,* 44 (1966/67), 205-222.

Though no formal use of HB is had, the A places some of its most typical statements in a most unambiguous position, especially through a development from later works. "One thing is sure. Man cannot make a misthought of Being, since it is Being itself which thinks his authentic thought..." (218). "The watchful shepherd of Being becomes Being's ventriloquist, his authentic piping of a divine gift given to him to distort or assist but not to originate".

Clearly, man is a mere instrument with no possible humanizing action. The A's interpretation is forcefully expressed but he moves forward too fast with one idea, neglecting any material or serious consideration (e.g., "Andenken") that does not already fall within his purview. His simple reference to a "mountain of literature on authentic thinking and thanking in modern phenomenology" is preposterous as is the addition, "For several of the better accounts related more or less directly to Heidegger, cf...", here follows a general reference to three of the most generic works except one which is a formidable treatise on SZ — all of which is left unsaid.

27. [C]   GRAFF, Frank de. *Het schuldprobleem in de existentiephilosophie van Martin Heidegger.* Boekencentrum N.V., 'S-Gravenhage, 1951, 161 pp.

The basic proposition is that H will call us back from an essentially ("zakelijk") materialistic metaphysics to religion; such a calling is "the hidden and most misunderstood ground of H's work" (48). The following logic (49-50) summarizes the A's approach: calling God the highest value is blasphemy [99], but God is Being; now, H seeks after Being, therefore God. It is confirmed by H's interpretation of Heraclitus' saying [108]. Though the A never takes up the distinction between "the God," "God", "the gods" nor alludes to the symbolic fabric of the background of H's interpretation, this text reappears in the final argument (111) as an acquired "proof". The A's interpretation is confirmed by the fact that H so adamently rejects the label of atheism. There is found, of course, the "Holy" argument (49). The question of the differences between Being and being is that of God and man (53): H thus posits the religious questions (68). According to such a context, the *êthos* of HB is the living in the nearness of God: the confrontation of man with Being is the vast ground of morality (111).

The interpretation is existentiel, theistic and theological. This book is an honest expression of an experience whose occasion, in part, was the reading of some passages from H. The mistake was to put "van Martin Heidegger" in the title; for, then, the A undertakes the dubious exercise of putting texts together without asking if they could bear the attributed meaning. The result is a simply disarming interpretation.

28. [B]   GUILEAD, Reuben. *Etre et liberté. Une étude sur le dernier Heidegger.* (Philosophes contemporains. Textes et études, 12) Louvain, Edit. Nauwelaerts; Paris, Béatrice-Nauwelaerts, 1965, 184 pp.

The HB and its question [esp. 94-100, 110] are set remarkably well within H's philosophy which is carefully read through the liberty thematic. This setting is positive but not simplistic; it shows that H is not to be confused with Hegel and that the HB is the consequence of the Reversal in which the overcoming of "humanism" is accomplished. Here we have the possibility of true authenticity, a realism mixed with a mystique, or a need of asceticism: man must be content and patient, humble and ready to walk in the nearness of Being. HB wishes to give the image of "homo humanus non metaphysicus". But there are unresolved questions; thus (175f), one may doubt in what sense this new humanism is concretely realizable since we know not what to think of the unresolved question of Being; still, HB is meant to be the new path. The question of its realization, or possibility thereof, should be left open.

Perhaps one should do the same with the A's interpretation. It is a "realistic" interpretation admitting unresolved, negative theology, language and "mysticism". Our reason for not placing it under the sign of "authenticity" is that his careful reservations at the end are not sufficiently underscored in relation to the intrinsic steps of his own undertaking. We believe they favor a "new way" that is more of a possibility than a reality, more of an ideal "mysticism" than something that can positively open upon such asceticism, humility, etc. required of the "new man".

29. [A]   HEINEMANN, F.H. *Existentialism and the Modern Predicament*. Harper Torchbooks, Harper & Brothers, Publishers, New York, 1958.

Within this survey, one of the best of its genre, a most knowledgeable A discusses briefly (95-101) H's thinking on values. H is essentially an anti-thinker ("Gegendenker"): both in metaphysics whose history is indiscriminately reduced to one of "essences" and in his thinking against values in which he violently overreacts against his training in the Windelband-Rickert-Münsterberg school. "Value" becomes but a creation of human subjectivity. The A cites a good portion of HB, 99/100 which "reveals his [H's] intention to 'think against' values together with the impossibility of doing so". Hence, "this thinking against values would seem to have catastrophic consequences for ethics".

The A's reasoning is solid but the nature of this work precludes his developing it more thoroughly just as it prevents us from making a closer evaluation.

30. [A]   HOMMES, Jakob. *Zwiespältiges Dasein. Die existenziale ontologie von Hegel bis Heidegger.* Verlag Herder, Freiburg i/B., 1953.

H, as the representative of "Existenzialphilosophie", is set within the dialectical development since Hegel of which he is the culmination. The light that could be thrown, however, on H's intent is quite dimmed by the A's thorough-going nihilistic interpretation and by the constant emphasis of the Godquestion polarizing the entire work on a "Split-Dasein" in terms of an "Existentialist-dialectical and a realistic-metaphysical philosophy" imposed on the text as an Aristotelian-Thomistic and realistic-theistic philosophy (348). Pp. 5-96 are on H with three-quarters of each page being a parallel book in fine print, a split book hard to read and replete with repetitiousness. Class-B would represent the A's reading of an "absolute humanism" but "A" must be chosen to designate H as the incarnate threat of the dialectic aimed at both human and divine values. Yet, the question of HB, as humanism and as ethics, is well set (19ff, 86ff) as a problematic, sc. the **negativity of the overcoming process and the absence of ethical categories in the concept of** *Existenz.*

31. [D]   HYLKEMA, G.W. *Homo Duplex. Het geweten als kern der ethiek.* Haarlem, de Erven F. Bohn N.V., 1963.

This volume must be mentioned in this main bibliography because it seems to pertain most explicitly to our subject (its main division being: Kant, Kant to Hegel, H, Kant to H, Hegel and H). In fact, it is not pertinent except perhaps as some historical background for, inspite of the subject-matter and abundant citations from H, there are only 5 passing references to HB (115, 139, 153, 160, 188) for all of which a parallel passage could just as well have been chosen. Rather astonishing in view of HB's consideration of ethic, law, etc. The index contains neither "grondethiek" nor "humanisme".

32. [D]   JASPERS, Karl. *Über Bedingungen und Möglichkeiten eines neuen Humanismus. Drei Vorträge.* Reclam [no. 8674], Stuttgart, 1962, 93 pp.

There is no question of considering H and Jaspers as interpreting one another but those familiar with the "special" relationship between these two original thinkers know that there are calcultated allusions to one another. In HB, the severe critique of the idea of Being as "Umfassende des Seienden" [26] employs one of Jaspers' cherished concepts, namely the "encompassing"; then, of course, "das 'Philosophieren' über das Scheitern..." [30] — a "philosophyzing" put between disdainful quotes — effectively describes Jaspers' thought.

Jaspers' "retort" in this work of 1949, slightly retouched in 1962, whose title for three different lectures is taken from the central and pertinent one (21-53) is more subtle and extensive. We have space to suggest only a few parallels: "Der erste Humanismus ist nicht der römische, sondern die griechische *Paideia* selbst (42) [cf. HB, 10-11: "Die so verstandene *paidéia*... in Rom begegnen wir den ersten Humanismus".]; on the tradition of humanism, Jaspers adds: "in seinem Boden wuchsen auch Hölderlin, Kierkegaard und Nietzsche" [cf. HB, 11: "Hölderlin dagegen gehört nicht in den "Humanismus"; on Nietzsche, cf. esp. 25]; "aus der Sorge um uns selbst" (23) [H's notion of "Sorge" und "Hirt"], "wenn wir zu uns selbst kommen" (27) [H's insistence on truth and Being as "ankommend"]; and in general the parallels "Selbstvergessenheit" ["Seinsvergessenheit"], "Verlorenheit" ["Heimlosigkeit"], "Technik", "Heil", "Verborgenheit", etc.

33. [D]   KING, Magda. *Heidegger's Philosophy. A Guide to his Basic Thought.* Macmillan. New York and Collier-Macmillan Limited, London, 1964. 193 pp. Also, Blackwell, Oxford, 1965.

In the initial part ("What is the Question") one finds the question on what it means to be man with reference to HB; yet, the A begs the question, concluding (181) that the upshot of SZ in the light of even late H is that "disclosure cannot happen to some abstract man in general, but only to a single, factually existing man". Though these later pages echo the words of HB there is no reference, let alone a prior development. The book never goes beyond the most often asserted basic structure of SZ. Granted that a basic guide has the difficult and thankless task of avoiding the simplistic and needless complications, it should not give the impression that H's questioning has not advanced at all since 1927.

34. [D]　KRAENZLING, G. *Existenzphilosophie und Panhumanismus*. Brunnen-Verlag. Schlehdorf am Kochelsee, 1950.

The value of this book is, for our purpose, quite singular: H's HB, like the works of other "existentialists", is studied as already inserted in an idealistic framework that contains its own key, if one recognizes its roots in a straightforward idealism. Undoubtedly, the A over-structures in view of presenting his own philosophy but he does give us reason to pause and consider the idealistic relationship of H's humanism. One cannot accept many an unstudied comparison: H's thought is explained in terms of Jaspers; Sartre's interpretation of SZ is the most obvious one, thus the correct one; after effectively limiting H to SZ, the A sees H's idealism as coming from Kierkegaard (234). For H, cf. 78-111; our question, esp. 110 f.

35a. [B]　KRÜGER, Gehard. "Martin Heidegger und der Humanismus". *Theologische Rundschau*, 18 (1950), 148-178. [Also, *Studia Philosophica* (Basel), 9 (1949), 93-129.]

This competent study is entirely pertinent (esp. 164 ff). We find restructured summaries of PW and of HB (complemented with WM), a "destruction" of H's reading of Plato, then a very well done critique — partly undone by being so devastating — of H's humanism as opening up on the crux of his entire thought. Taking a modern view, H reads back into Plato, most un-Platonically. He comes up with a mishmash ["ein unfruchtbare Bastard"] of ancient theological and modern subjectivistic thinking. The A maintains that H confuses the Good and the "really real" with Plato's "humanism", and, thus, the question of "value" in HB. H clearly attempts to create a "new" humanism and not some mere "anti-ism". The A indicates in what sense Plato and H's interpretation, and H himself, are "humanist". Though H has no case *historisch,* a mediating rôle of man can humanize Being's relation. But H deals really with a meta-humanism and, *nolens, volens,* a crass humanizing of Being.

For a calm, balanced judgement of the meaning of humanism, cf. 171-72. The A has weakened his extremely well reasoned case by not bringing to bear his analysis of the *Kehre* or of a norm of sense (Sinn) at the crucial point of H's "dichotomy" which, perhaps, would then not be as blatant as it appears.

35b. *Grundfragen der Philosophie: Geschichte, Wahrheit, Wissenschaft.* Vittorio Klostermann, Frankfurt am Main, 1958. 288 pp.

This volume is based on a series of lectures (1942-52) without indicating, however, the date of its parts. The added notes refer one occasionally to the above article. Though only a dozen pages are formally given to H, the A's severe criticism of H's "humanism" is seen as part of the general field of a fundamental problematic of philosophy and its history. We have a vaulable context for seeing, as it were, the Heideggerian phenomenon. Cf. esp. 210-11.

36. [C] LANGAN, Thomas. *The Meaning of Heidegger. A Critical Study of an Existentialist Phenomenology.* Columbia University Press, New York (also London), 1959. 247 pp.

This work has the merit of presenting in clear, and often forceful language the pure position of authentic humanism; unfortunately, however, it is an *uncritical* reflection. The whole thought of H is harmoniously interpreted as a personalist philosophy of life with no problems, either *historisch* or *geschichtlich.* The ethical and humanistic question, however, is explicitated with considerable interest (e.g., 40, 173, 209). The A's critique is in effect put off to the end as an appendaged "attack" launched, ironically, from traditionalist ground; were it seriously incorporated, the book's thesis would be intrinsically untenable. Furthermore, no serious consideration of any opposing opinion is made, nor any use of those prior works (even some of those in his bibliography) which could have given this book less of a preaching tone and more that of a reasoned, reflected experience. Adding the fact that the A betrays severe shortcomings with the German language, let alone H's, as manifested by many indefensible translations according to any norm of interpretation, it becomes quite impossible within this space to suggest a detailed critique.

LLAMBIAS DE AZEVEDO, Juan. Cf. AZEVEDO, no. 6.

37a. [A] LÖWITH, Karl. "Heideggers 'Kehre' ". *Die neue Rundschau,* 62, (1951), H. 4, 48-79.

This most knowledgeable early student of H's provides such a competent catalogue of the changes in H's thought, which, for the A, amounts to an "about-face" on H's part, that this article has become a classic statement of such a position, being tightly argued and lightened with humor, irony and sarcasm. H's new course leaves no room for the human factor as a consequence of the "Topology of Being" (76) in which Dasein no longer can open up the sense (Sinn) of Being. For "Ethos" in HB, cf. p. 49. If one reads H thus, it is difficult to fault the argumentation.

37b. HEIDEGGER. *Denker in dürftiger Zeit.* 3., durchgesehene Auflage. Vandenhoeck & Ruprecht in Göttingen, 1965. 112 pp. [Kleine Vandenhoeck-Reihe, no. 98/99].

This work, a classic of its genre, expands the above, working it throughout H's philosophy. It provides all the ammunition that one would reasonably require for considering HB's protest against the misunderstanding of H's own thought as one really revealing more readily the very shortcomings thereof. For our purpose, however, the above article remains more concisely focused on our question.

38. [A] Lukacs, Georg. "Heidegger Redivivus". *Sinn und Form* (Potsdam-Berlin), 1 (1949), 3. H, 37-62.

Writing in terms of HB, the A sees H trying a "third way" between the idealist and the materialist. This way becomes a "subjective idealism" (49) and a contradiction which is refuted as such (esp. 59-60) and in part by showing the practical and economic exigencies of reality over against H's "subjectivistic utopia" — which, we may add, would be the very nature of his new "humanism". The interesting analyses of HB, such as humanism (38) and the argumentation in favor of a "pure anthropology" (48) are offset, unfortunately, by the strength of the diatribe against H. HB is the "first post-fascist" work and any reinterpretation or self-interpretation is cast aside because H remains trapped in the old framework, just as he continues living in a "Monopolkapitalismus" experiencing the pathos of the nihilism of despair.

Undoubtedly, this interpretation has more than one adherent and should be read as a sort of classic of this type, omitting the few passages lacking all interest due to insistent repetition — e.g., one finds eight times, in the space of less than one page, the word "fascist" and its compounds cemented by appropriate Marxist categories. — On the relationship between the A and H, cf. no. 5, pp. 8-9.

39. [C] Macomber, William B. *The Anatomy of Disillusion. Martin Heidegger's Notion of Truth.* Northwestern University Press, Evanston, 1967. 227 pp.

This eminently readable volume, well thought out in English, fulfills its introductory aim with an existentialistic interpretation in the constant light of SZ. Though the A choses to develop only H's "phenomenology", he states that it gives rise to "a host of recommendations for being human, his existentialism". HB, 104-19 shows that "H is not concerned with elaborating any particular criterion of conduct in an attempt to establish a theory of value. He wants rather to explain the possibility of a criterion as such, whatever it may be." (97).

The book's virtue is also its defect. "...the two parts of his philosophy are actually unthinkable *except* in conjunction" (8); unfortunately, the A's intended reader would not suspect that there are indeed two parts. "...my study is meant to be introductory. It stops short of the question which must figure prominently in any final assessment of H as a thinker". This bracketing process is used legitimately in the positive exposition though it yields a thought too perfectly harmonious; it is quite illegitimate, however, to dispatch summarily some of the best known interpreters for reasons that could only depend upon the very questions the A has bracketed and it is no feat to demolish someone with the crux of the problem unmentioned (e.g., 113 f). Furthermore, the process leads to needless confusion: the A insists on capitalizing "Being" only for the last works of H, yet writes "being" with appended multiple footnote references with early and late works, just as he refutes some by using texts appearing after the publication of the work in question.

40a. [C] MARX, Werner. "Heidegger's New Conception of Philosophy. The Second Phase of 'Existentialism'". *Social Research* (New York), 22 (1955), 451-474.

This clear and competent study by H's successor at Freiburg explicitly proposes a definite interpretation: the final overcoming of the remnants of "Cartesianism", whose last stage is set by HB. An authentic approach is opened at once to both man and Being because of "the identity of the Da of Being and of man" (465). "The Second, or New Approach", regains the real setting of man and of Being and thereby is articulated "a new 'Essence of Man'" (453) — in effect, a new humanism. This new opening is a pre-Socratic awareness of man as an "instrument of Being".

As it appears from the last page, this approach is limited to the few, indeed to the elite, or better the elected ones of which H is the present-day prophetic utterance. With due respect to this study's coherency within its basic adherence to H, it is far from convincing. The magnitude of the philosophical problems raised by stressing the "identity of the Da" are not set aside by the simple statements: "[it] does not rob man of his entire status" and "the new philosopher feels himself again as intermediary, instrument and voice". The A "assumes" *the* condition for "authentic humanism" within this framework, namely, that the overcoming-process has come off. The many questions that come to a reader's critical reflection are merely touched upon by the volume below:

40b.   *Heidegger und die Tradition. Eine problemgeschichtliche Einführung in die Grundbestimmungen des Seins*. W. Kohlhammer Verlag, Stuttgart, 1961. 268 pp.

The A compares H's notion of Being with a tradition from Aristotle to Hegel which has been [supposedly] fixed on essence. If one compares the question of man's rôle (146, 239, 242) with ethics (118f, 241), the A is aiming at *how* and why man can come to stand in the truth of Being and be ethical (sc., be human). Thus some unavoidable HB-questions are put into sharp focus. The question, however, on the origin of good and evil (ethical) (243ff, 154) seems imposed; furthermore, in developing H's ambiguity, the A confuses Da-sein, Mensch and Menschen*wesen*. Too strongly influenced by H's idea of history, the A's critique is an appendage to a series of summaries. "It" is "difficult" "to read" his "intention" — quite seriously, because the par per page of expressions within quotation marks is 24.

41. [C]   Masi, Giuseppe. *La Libertà in Heidegger (Ricerche sulla sua filosofia)*. Nicola Zanichelli, Bologna, 1961 196 pp.

The *Handeln* of HB, 5 is the action through which man tends to realize himself completely in a kind of consenting process ("un 'consentire' "); liberty in the metaphysical sense "reveals itself as the essence of all true *humanism*" (111f) — and here follows a good development of "Ek-sistenz". H's entire philosophy, as Spinoza's, is like an ethic, an axiological metaphysics guaranteed on the plane of epochal history and sustained by the very necessity of Being (160). "Authenticity is value by the simple fact that it means the totality of human being as truth and liberty"; "being is person in so far it makes itself person" ("in quanto *si fa* persona" (162).

The exposition is clear and certainly knowledgeable but sufficiently tinged with Heideggerian jargon that the problematic is often untouched; there is scarcely a difference between the exposition and the "observations". The entire approach assumes a real reciprocity of action in H (cf. 124f); hence, there is no difficulty in arriving at the notion of person. Furthermore, two planes of thought are mixed in giving us a type of Kierkegaardian authenticity (163). Stated in fine print at the end (192) is the *fact* that the interpretation of H's humanism is still unresolved; yet, the book has proceeded as if it were. The A should have given us hints along the way; otherwise, the appended note places his work under the unexamined "Spiel des Seins".

42. [B]   Morra, Gianfranco. "Essenzialismo di Martin Heidegger". *Giornale critico della filosofia italiana*, 32 (1953), 363-70.

HB describes man's task as a continuous search after Being, conceived as the One of Plotinus. Man must stand in the light of Being but this is like trying to get out of Plato's cave by contemplating the singular existent; man finds himself homeless (Heimatlosigkeit) since his true homeland is the One. H's philosophy, especially in the light of recent writings, is stripped of what any real existentialism should possess: the exigency — even if it be unrealizable — of grounding an effective liberty of the person. The obstacle of Being paralyzes all free action and makes ethics impossible.

Granted the article's conciseness, there is still too much dependence on secondary sources and a lack of reasoning on HB; but the foundations for a good case are well implied. The A, we believe, overstresses his difference with Chiodi (no. 17a).

43. [C]   MÜLLER, Max. *Existenzphilosophie im geistigen Leben der Gegenwart*. 3., wesentlich erweiterte und verbesserte Auflage. F.H. Kerle Verlag, Heidelberg, 1964. 299 pp.

The entire first half of this volume bears most directly on our subject since it had been basically presented at Freiburg under the title "Martin Heideggers Humanismus-Brief", a fact that explains the numerous quoted expressions without mention of HB as source. Since the central thesis is that H is an outstanding example of the Western tradition of philosophy, specifically of Judeo-Greek-Christian thought, and since a central part is given to HB, it follows that H's thought on humanism and ethics would be most faithful to this same tradition. Though this is the unexpressed bare logic, it permeates the book as it is quite clear (e.g., 212) that HB exemplifies this tradition by opening *positively* upon value, the ethical and Christian humanism — notwithstanding the somewhat cautionary foonote, p. 85.

With a firm background of traditional philosophy and theology, the A presents a very consistent and highly intelligible case. When one recognizes H's own admission of indebtedness to theology — at least as to its language — the A's concern for a continuity of Thomistic philosophy (139, 180) cannot be readily dismissed. Granting his purpose, we find the A's own thought not sufficiently marked off from his exposition of H. The position is markedly "class-C" because of the context out of which it is read; the question remains how much of this context is read into H. On the ethic question, cf. 85ff, in conjuction with ontological guilt, cf. 48 and with the basic question of how "Da-sein" can be (sc., the very possibility of any humanism) cf. 42.

44a. [C]   PAUMEN, Jean. "Heidegger et le sens du chemin". *Revue de l'Université de Bruxelles*, 17 (1965), 384-425.

This skillful and accurate development through H's "turnings" (from SZ, 165 to US) on the long continuous march through language into the fullness of silence graced with awareness of the bond, man-Being, that now accounts for the formerly stressed exigences of man (e.g., resolution), is admirably Heideggerian. Along this way, man's changing, if not diminishing, rôle is clearly underlined in function of his relation to history which *is* Being's.

The whole tenor of this undertaking appears real and authentic since one supposes a real "existentiel" content for the described structure. But the abundant references to HB are quickly taken up into H's pure concern for pure language. Thus the difficult question of man's rôle comes clearly to the fore but never a wayward step is taken from the self-consistent and self-generative vocabulary of H to ask what historical reality is here after all.

44b. "Heidegger et le thème nietzschéen de la mort de Dieu". *Revue internationale de philosophie*, 52 (1960) 238-262.

Within this good treatment for a famous theme, the A's suppositions for our C-classification become clear. After considering man's rôle in HW and esp. in HB, 66, 67, 75, he states that there is in effect a new theory of participation — we would say, "humanism", since this word may be less objectionable to H. We hesitate, however, to use this article to clarify the one above, because there the A never refers to this one though the occasions are abundant, almost compelling. Could it be that he had in the meantime undergone the impact of US?

45. [A] PFLAUMER, Ruprecht. "Sein und Mensch im Denken Heideggers". *Philosophische Rundschau,* 13 (1966), 161-234.

This scholarly, searching study looks for the human factor "in the question left open": the unity of Being, man and beings in the Event" (222). What rôle is had for man with beings (229) when one considers the very structure of his thinking and willing (172, 209)? Humanism is a particular anthropology (170). If man is presence of Being, he must *also* be a presence with beings, if he is a relation to Being's language, he must *also* be an awareness, a body, an I, a willing and acting being; if he is the "place of Being", he must be some kind of participating member (167, 221). (For "also", cf. "zugleich", 202, 228, 229, 232). H has over-desubjectivized because the essence of the I character of man is not grounded in "metaphysics" but vice versa (202).

Though the logic of this analysis leaves perhaps no way for H to "save man", the A brings to it some mitigating, though somewhat extrinsic, questions. Strangely, without giving notice, he moves from the meaning of "entsprechen" which could only have been that of "corresponding" on p. 173 (and hence merely "structural") to that of "answering" (221). Since 170ff posits the overcoming of a "metaphysical humanism" and the rest of the study searches for the reality that is man's along side the fundamental relation of Being, the *entire* study is most pertinent and illuminating by asking questions that must be asked.

46a. [C] PÖGGELER, Otto. *Der Denkweg Martin Heideggers.* Verlag Günther Neske Pfullingen, 1963, 318 pp.

Among works sympathetic to H, this is perhaps unquestionably the most intelligent, systematic reflection. It presents his thought as a way of thinking in view of the fundamental question, and quest, of Being. All the more important factors, historical and personal, plus many an unpublished mss., are brought to bear. This work puts the HB in context, it appears at a crucial juncture (259). Man is thematized only in so far as he is the being necessary for the history of manifestation, sc., of truth, that is, of Being. H does not exclude questions pertaining to man and to society since one must first find the ground (Boden) on which these questions should be posited (260). On the centrality of HB, cf. 104 which makes difficult any mere apologetic interpretation; on *êthos,* cf. 205; on the ethical, cf. 286. — unfortunately, there is no index.

The A assumes as valid H's fondamental outlook. Concrete questioning on man is put off just as the God-question: we must await for the language to arise or (merely ?) come to us. Granted that H may be testifying to a fundamental approach, the A's tone betrays a "faith" in H's way: the nearly exclusive interest in Being and its Doing will some day permit the removal of the brackets around man's doing. He speaks with H of a "daring" (Wagnis, 286) but *who* posits such an act, if ever? For us, at least, a central problem of HB comes to the fore: will this approach, with its little real "content" be capable of being fleshed-out or has it already plunged us too far into "the relation of Being" who initiates all, and perhaps does all? But for such questioning, the A gives a valuable insight: H's way is not an ideal nor a program but a way without specific content (187).

46b. "Metaphysik und Seinstopik bei Heidegger". *Philosophisches Jahrbuch,* 70 (1962), 118-137.

Those who are anxious to give an anthropological interpretation or are eager to see a "subjectivism" should consider the contrary arguments.

46c. "Existenziale Anthropologie". In: *Die Frage nach dem Menschen. Aufriss einer philosophischen Anthropologie.* Festschrift für Max Müller zum 60. Geburtstag. Herausgegeben von Heinrich Rombach. Verlag Karl Alber, Freiburg/München, 1966, pp. 443-60.

For a positive, concise treatment of an existential anthropology as a basic outline for a philosophical anthropology.

47a. [D] RICHARDSON, Willian J. *Heidegger. Through Phenomenology to Thought.* Preface by M. HEIDEGGER. M. Nijhoff, The Hague, 1963. 764 pp.

No doubt the best work in English and, in any language, the finest instrument for a coming to the text of H. It is *not* a study *on* H and in keeping with his purpose, the A's thought, though often clearer than the original, reveals, through its faithfulness, the same basic ambiguity as H's; as such, it is scarcely a help to our HB question. One should note, however, the A's explicitation of H's intention in view of a "humanism of a higher kind" (though the statement is softened as a question, p. 552) whose conception goes "beyond humanism" (531) in the traditional sense of man's nature. For an accurately, highly Heideggerian summary on "humanism", cf. 387-90, for HB, 530-52; for the link of HB with prior thought, 46 and with PW, 387 ff.

47b. "Heidegger and the Quest of Freedom". *Theological Studies*, 28 (1967), 286-307.

The nature of this article allows the A to give a somewhat more explicit lead as to our subject, though it is couched as a possible "inspiration" rather than interpretation. As far as H is concerned, we have absolutely no right to transpose any of his early thought into morality (297) "but as such, it remains an ontological condition of possibility for moral action" (SZ, 286); as for "Heidegger-II" [to which belongs the HB period], he is "no more concerned with morality than Heidegger-I" (303) — though the reader might wish to know if he is any less concerned. For a summary of the notion of ethics according to HB, cf. 303-05 which emphasizes the text's linking of "foundational thinking" and original ethics.

47c. "Heidegger and the Problem of Thought". *Revue philosophique de Louvain*, 60 (1962), 58-78.

The relation of foundational thought to metaphysics is like that to technicity, logic and humanism. Hence, if the positive intention of overcoming metaphysics is seen (e.g., 69) with the treatment of metaphysics in this article, then we would venture to say that H's attack on "humanism" is clarified as to its intention.

48. [B] RINTELEN, Fritz-Joachim. *Philosophie der Endlichkeit als Spiegel der Gegenwart*. Westkulturverlag Anton Hain, Meisenheim/Glan, 1951. 490 pp.

In examining the question on how man can again become man, the A sees in HB's conception of man as the "there" and the "clearing of Being", a distinct idealism. The reality of Being fulfills itself (159) while the structure of Being remains ontologically inaccessible. For man stands in Being's clearing as neither a who nor a what, neither a person nor an object (158); finally (421), his *Ek-sistenz* is taken up, subsumed, in and by an a-personal Being where appear both an I-Being ("Ich-Sein überhaupt") as "Will to Power" and a romantic, or better, a Hegelian trait.

Though the A's interpretation is clear, it is hard to arrive at because of his effort to make at the same time his own "overcoming" of existentialism. Never staying long enough with a given author, he indulges in indiscrete linking of thinkers, though, it must be added, scarcely ever without interest. Thus, in a formal section of a few pages on H, he speaks of Jaspers, Barth, Rilke, Augustine, Pascal, etc. such that it resembles any other section of the book. H is threaded throughout the entire work, helping its unity under a tension, since the A is preoccupied with the religious and Christian questions. Accordingly, HB is generally passim (35-446) and thoroughly passim 73-101, 158-212, and 282-306.

49. [D] ROSTENNE, Paul. "L'Ontologie entravée de Heidegger". *Revue de métaphysique et de morale,* 71 (1966), 74-99.

The question on humanism arises in the light of the entire movement of H's thought and of the vacuous death of metaphysical, theological and religious thought-experience. In this very tightly and excellently argued framework, the key to the unity and consistency is H's notion of "temporality" *in* which the "ecstatic inhabitation" defines an ontocentric *humanitas*: a "natural" humanism which is not trans-natural because its fulfilment is in *human* thought and in one's contribution to the final realization of the authentic thought of Being. Humanism, as synthesized in HB, expresses precisely the approach towards being in the nearness of Being, it does not allow for an idea of "communion" — and in esp. this last point, one finds serious reasons that many a critique has failed to consider, though the A's idea about an approach in finite tension towards an impossible union would suggest to us Jaspers. The context of this study suggests different levels for reading H's "humanism"; thus, it precludes any short summary attempting to classify the interpretation.

50. [A] Ruiz de Elvira, Antonio. "Humanismo y sobrehumanismo. Heidegger y San Pablo. *Revista de la Universidad de Madrid,* 2 (1953), 165-193.

The core critique is incisive in respect to H's intention which the A has well grasped ("Este humanitismo, antihumanismo o más-que-humanismo, pues se presenta como el deseo de fundar un humanismo más auténtico", 187). Coming from a classical background, he finds that all forms of humanism have historically one minimal common denominator: an emphasis on man that excludes his need for opening up on any other higher being, specifically God. To this notion he opposes "sobrehumanismo" — an unfortunately intruding expression. Since H thinks in terms of non-nihilism, non-atheism, non-destruction-of-values, and, above all, non-indifferentism, his thinking is purely humanistic. The interpretation belongs to class-B but because H's anti-humanism is identified with the very humanism that he himself condemns, we have class-A.

Though this article attempts too much, the core critique built up from HB does meet H insipte of very serious shortcomings e.g., the critique of language neglects its "phenomenological" usage; the argument for "pure reason" alone, as capable of setting the limit for enunciating thought as neither theistic nor atheistic, should at least consider the famous passage "Erst aus...". We find hastily imposed categories and though the idea of two limiting cases is excellent (sc., H. and Paul who is mentioned only symbolically) it should have been developed elsewhere. The sub-title is deceptive; it would have been better to start the article no earlier than p. 173 — H is 185ff.

51. [B]   SCHLAWIN, Hermann. "Heideggers Überwindung der Metaphysik". *Zeitschrift für philosophische Forschung*, 8 (1954), 585-95.

The A presents a well argued critique of the very possibility of H's approach. For, how can one know when one has arrived at "original" thought ? How can one say whether he is in or out of metaphysical thinking — given the pervasiveness of such thinking ? Is not that thinking described as taken up by Being's own relating activity still metaphysical ? Then should not HB, 7 (in effect: das Denken gehört dem Sein) mean that Being thinks itself in the thinking proposed by H ("...es [das Sein] denkt im Denken sich selbst") ? Yet, H's entire approach to humanism depends on the successful overcoming of metaphysics.

52. [D]   SCHWAN, Alexander. *Politische Philosophie im Denken Heideggers*. "Ordo Politicus", 2. Bd. Westdeutscher Verlag, Köln und Opladen, 1965. 206 pp.

The line-up (10) of the notions of political philosophy and philosophical work-analysis (esp. with reference to "Handlung", HB, 5) as well as H's interpretation of the truth of Being (12) linked to "ethics" are promising. But after considering "êthos" (56) in terms of "struggle" and "repetition", and restating H's notion on ethos as "sojourn" and "place" (61); ethics [HB, 38ff], the A observes, is a narrowing down of the question of man's essential place ("Wesenort") in relation to Being, which, becoming identified with "ontology", is taken up ("aufgehoben") in favor of H's reflection on the essence of truth. This book is indeed very well correlated but not proportionately profound. Its bibliography is outstanding.

53a. [B]   USCATESCU, George. "El humanismo de Martin Heidegger". *Revista de filosofía* (Madrid), 17 (1958), 459-69 [cf. also *Revista de la Universidad nacional de Córdoba*, same year].

H has always been preoccupied with a philosophical anthropology which has simply shifted into the fundamental ontology question in which man finds his "place" as Being's referent. The minimum content of the new humanism is that "man has, as his mission, to lend his ear to the voice of Being", an attitude "que tiene mucho de religioso". Though there is not lacking the "tension" of concrete situations reminiscent of *Lebensphilosophie;* nevertheless, H's thought is relegated to an "absolute and pure zone", adiabatic to ethical implications and, indeed, impervious to the plane on which his critics find themselves.

Unfortunately, this interpretation is merely tacked on to the end of the A's exposition which is most *un*clear, especially because one cannot readily differentiate his thought from perplexing paraphrasings without specific references — usually, the latter are somewhat clearer. The A proceeds from the "anthropology" of KM directly to HB, mentioning Plato and omitting PW! The article is marred by the A's over-preoccupation with H's supposedly perennial preoccupation with anthropology.

53b.   "El humanismo de Martin Heidegger". In: *Escatología e Historia.* Ediciones Guadarrama, Madrid, 1959, pp. 145-161.

This is the same material as the article above, slightly retouched. It has sufficiently more clarity to reassure us of our above judgement.

53c.   "Humanismo y técnica en Martin Heidegger". Universidad Internacional Menéndez Pelayo, Santander, 1961. 15 pp. [Also, *Crisis* (Madrid), 7 (1960), 89-103].

Quoting abundantly without specific references, the A fails to take up any problematic. Perhaps some light is shed by his easy moving through H's works in function of a "neohumanism" that requires an evaluation of modern man's technicity. The A extolls the *concept* of "Shepherd of Being" as heralding a new humanism.

We cannot honestly find sufficient grounds for the multiple diffusion of these articles.

54. [C]   VÀTTIMO, Gianni. *Essere, storia e linguaggio in Heidegger*. Edizioni di "Filosofia", Torino, 1963. 202 pp.

The subject of humanism occasioned an expression of the *Kehre* that should have been Part Three of SZ. By a shift of accent from man to Being, HB appears resolutely anti-humanistic but *only* in the metaphysical view. This *Kehre* is the ontological repetition of the analytic [SZ] reversing metaphysics and humanism in order to escape their language-concepts. Language is the only way to repeat ontologically; man's existence is repeated as Being as Event, where he is the way to Being, its place of *Er-örterung*. History is not humanistic, it is Being's; it is a dialogue where language contains the mystery of the relation man-Being. *Geschick*, as call-response, is its key; true history is that of language. Man is man authentically only in language. Thus, the title of the book represents the progression of H's way: Being, History, Language. Cf. esp. 105-112; also, 4-8, 142, 162, 186-92.

This unusually intelligible presentation clearly posits the question; its interpretation of the reversal as absorbing "humanism" into the question of the history and language of Being is well argued such that there is really no need to take HB as some "occasion". True dialogue is assumed. Indeed, this may perhaps be H, but we would have liked to see some of the main difficulties interpreted.

55. [A]   VERSÉNYI, Laszlo. *Heidegger, Being and Truth*. Yale University Press, New Haven and London, 1965. 201 pp.

"SZ was humanistic in intention" but not sufficiently humanistic in its outcome to point towards authenticity; "the last writings attempt to offer a way of salvation that has no humanistic aim and is, therefore, impossible for man to follow" (187). In overcoming humanistic ethics, H "overextends the existential onto-theological demand of human nature (for continued self-transcendence) into a demand for absolute transcendence, and thus winds up with an empty, totally negative notion of transcendent existence..."; H "closes his thinking on a radically nihilistic note" (195).

This work is an extensive treatment of our subject that could have been entitled "Human and Non-Human Understanding in H". The index makes easy a study of the HB-aspects. A clear presentation purports to show that the human question has been suppressed; a much better case would have been made, had the A considered more seriously H's self-interpretations (e.g., those opposing SZ's "humanistic intention" and the nihilistic view) and especially if he had not ignored the notion of the "holy" in his critique of transcendence.

56a. [C] VIETTA, Egon. "Being, World and Understanding. A Commentary on Heidegger" (trsl. by Susanne JUNGBAUER). *Review of Metaphysics*, 5 (1951/2), 157-72.

This compact, comprehensive laying-out of H's fundamental effort makes available in English an ideal setting for HB. Though this is not the A's intention, it happens from the fact of its centrality. In HB all consideration for the hitherto accepted metaphysical notion of man has been dropped and the thinking proceeds from the "Being of Da-sein", metaphorically speaking, from "above" (165): 158 ff describe that type of thinking against which HB reacts; 166ff that type of thinking at which it is aiming, sc., Being comprehending itself in man "in a new way which unveils Being". "In the last analysis man *is* Thinking inasmuch as 'Being' thinks itself in him (which is also the reason why man has the key to the understanding of Being)".

But, nowhere, in this newly elevated man, do we find room for asking the naïve question whether man has a real human or personal rôle in this process.

56b. *Die Seinsfrage bei Martin Heidegger.* Schwab, Stuttgart, 1950. 146 pp.

The A, a faithful disciple of H, makes an imaginative exposition of the more essential, or at least, the most salient themes. HB, and its questioning are not developed, though the Letter is called "eine Gesamtdeutung seines Philosophierens"

(29). Of some pertinence would be the reading of "Gewissen und Ethik", 115ff.

57. [C] VYCINAS, Vincent. *Earth and Gods. An Introduction to the Philosophy of Martin Heidegger.* Nijhoff, The Hague, 1961. 326 pp.

Primary thinking [HB, 6] is not "irrational" in the context of deontologized thought. For human thought is not simply human since it does not fully belong to man, nor is it "logical"; H thinks Being and not beings (77, 109). This is authenticity. The crucial text, "Das Sein kommt, sich lichtend zur Sprache" [45], means that "Being needs human words, wherein, as authentic language, it dwells, it spells itself out" (86f). Nature (phýsis) has been misunderstood, it is the unity of H's thought: it means the "ultimate essence of thinking and talking" (149), man's responses are merely that of logos, the language of Being; hence, to let be (89) constitutes the History of Being. Thus the question of "value" [35] is "letting nature be the way it is laid and articulated in itself" (98).

It becomes abundantly clear what would be a key significance of the positive overcoming of "humanism". Between what we would call "structural" and "existentiel" thinking the A moves smoothly in a flowing restatement of H. Once on the latter plane, it is too late to ask the petty questions of life's stage. Through an unquestioned, real content of H's "correspondence" (Entsprechen), we have here a truly consistent position. The A's own translations, though often very good, make it difficult at times to recapture H's precise thought, especially without the German in note.

58. [C] WIPLINGER, Fridolin. *Wahrheit und Geschichtlichkeit. Eine Untersuchung über die Frage nach dem Wesen der Wahrheit im Denken Martin Heideggers.* Verlag Karl Alber, Freiburg/München, 1961. 386 pp.

HB is treated within the framework of the A's central question of the "Kehre" such that the main proposition of a "new" kind of thinking is clearly exemplified by HB. Apparently, the

New Way would be equivalent to HB's intent (309-10) in conformity with the continuity of the Daseins-analysis that necessarily opens upon this way. We also have a statement on the "ethos" of the "ethik" (356, cf. 365).

The A's wish to make no criticism (9) should not, however, excuse his uncritical acceptance of H's Way, nor his ceaseless paraphrasing culminating on p. 317 as "our interpretation" where one is still at a loss to see what he has brought, nor, finally, his free progression from the ontological to the "theological difference". Asking what is "this new essential thinking", i.e., "the authentic thinking of the Kehre", the A conjures up "metanoein" (328-9) followed by a series of de facto unprepared statements constituting a complete personalist philosophy (331); these statements allow him to speak of "Dies Konsequenz..." (*ibid*.) from which point he is completely free to move on — which he does, often with keen insights but insufficient time or space to knit them.

59. [D]   WYSCHOGROD, Michael. *Kierkegaard and Heidegger. The Ontology of Existence*. Routledge & Kegan Paul Ltd. London [And: Humanitas Press, New York], 1954, 156 pp.

Hightened by the contrast Kierkegaard-H, early and middle H, the A's question of how to combine the "existential" and ontological approaches belongs to our HB reading. A thought shift marks the start of humanism (118) but H's own thinking is "subjective" (133); HB, 99-100 is against the "view that places reality on one level and then proceeds, by means of experience, to add value to reality"; later H is "non-existentialistic" in maintaining "the concept of Being in its independence and the understanding of the human situation in the light of man as the medium of the revelation of Being" (120).

Granting the insight to be gained by polarizing a book between two thinkers, the dangers are evident: oversimplification is expected but not the imposition and facile transposition of categories nor the omission of basic notions found even in the very works analyzed (e.g., *Entsprechen, Ereignis*) in order to arrive at summary contrasts (120). Unfortunately, there is added a lack of clarity due to sentence structures and the literal translation of German structure (e.g., PW, 49 on p. 118). Coupled with the confusion of the A's own intertwined categories, our reading does not permit us to wager a classification.

COMPLEMENTARY BIBLIOGRAPHY

60.   BECK, A. "Hölderlin". In: *Die Religion in Geschichte und Gegenwart*. Dritte, völlig neu bearbeitete Auflage, JCB Mohr (Paul Siebeck), Tübingen, 1959, 3. Bd., 394-98.

For a concise treatment of the rôle of the poet as conceived by Hölderlin, cf. this article whose striking parallel not only in expression but also in conception to Heidegger's idea of the thinker, as found in HB, will not go unnoticed.

61.   BECK, Ernst Ludwig. "Der ontologische Imperativ. Hoffentlich ein Beitrag zum Verständnis Martin Heideggers". *Wissenschaft und Weltbild*, 8 (1955), 206-12.

The A claims to put H into normal German to make especially one point which has supposedly been neglected: thinking (Denken) and Being are so united in *Sagen* that there is no commanding necessity. Though there is not much developed thereof, this article does in fact pertain to HB's ethical question [esp. 44-5].

62.   BEYER, W.R. "Herr Heidegger — und die Friedensfrage". *Deutsche Zeitschrift für Philosophie* (E. Berlin), 10 (1962), 1533-53.

H is still the Fascist of old and such is the tenor of the call sounded by HB, specifically p. 119. The main part of the article is adequately described by the formidable sub-heading: "Heideggers 'Kehre' als Widerspiegelung der 'Kehre' des Nationalsozialismus zum Neo- und Klerikalfaschismus".

63.   BOCK, Irmgard. *Heideggers Sprachdenken.* (Monographien zur philosophischen Forschung, Bd. 40). Verlag Anton Hain, Meisenheim am Glan, 1966, 117 pp.

This book is not directly pertinent unless we ask whether humanism is definable in terms of language, then a reflection on the centrality of HB described as the culmination of the poet-interpretation period (72) should become very englightening.

64.   BUBER, M. "Religion und modernes Denken". *Merkur* (Stuttgart), 6 (1952), 101-20.

For a quite different appreciation than, for example, Pöggeler's, on the God-question and HB [85f, 102f] cf.pp. 106-108.

65.   CHAIX, Ruy, J. "Humanisme: transcendance de l'humain". *Giornale di metafisica*, 7 (1952), 647-660.

An interesting article on the generic crisis of humanism. Of particular interest is the notion of the past in the present joined with a search for total experience; here, H's existent is "suspended in the void" (649).

66.   CORETH, Emerich. "Das fundamentalontologische Problem bei Heidegger und Hegel". *Scholastik*, 29 (1954), 1-23.

This article gives an historical context to HB in terms of Hegel (as others do esp. in terms of Kant, e.g., no. 6) by an A qualified to speak on both philosophers. Cf. esp. p. 7.

67.   Demske, James M. *Sein, Mensch und Tod. Das Todesproblem bei Martin Heidegger.* Verlag Karl Alber, Freiburg/München, 1963, 207pp.

For a remarkably incisive summary statement of the meaning and motive of the "Kehre", cf. 111-12; and for the famous text "Erst aus der Wahrheit des Seins... nennen soll", cf. 130n.

68a.   FABRO, Cornelio. "Ontologia dell'arte nell'ultimo Heidegger". *Giornale critico della filosofia italiana,* 31(1952), 344-61.

H's critique of the history of metaphysics, to which belongs humanism, is sympathetically summarized by one most competent to put it in its true historical perspective. For our purpose, this highly packed article is more directly pertinent than the volume below.

68b.   *Dall'essere all'esistente.* Marcelliana, Brescia, 1957. 521 pp.

H is esp. treated 337-424; the essential points of the above article are taken up. Of great interest is the rich historical context, particularly in relation to Kant, 349ff; Schelling, 384ff, and the God-question, 400ff.

69.   FUNKE, Gerhard. "Ethos: Gewohnheit, Sitte, Sittlichkeit". *Archiv für Rechts- und Sozialphilosophie* (Berlin), 47 (1961), 1-80.

This study is in large measure an historical survey whose first pages (especially 3-5) in treating of the Greek notion of *êthos* are evidently pertinent to our question; a later reference to H (65), though of interest, is too generic.

70a.   GADAMER, Hans-Georg. *Wahrheit und Methode.* 2. Aufl. J.C.B. Mohr (Paul Siebeck), Tübingen, 1965.

Within the full, rich context of the hermeneutical question (94ff) one finds H's critique of subjectivism and the overcoming process thereof, which is so central to the HB-question. For a very pointed critique of Bollnow, cf. 248.

70b.   "Über die Möglichkeit einer philosophischen Ethik". In: *Sein und Ethos. Untersuchungen zur Grundlegung der Ethik.* Herausgegeben von P. Engelhardt. Matthias-Grünewald-Verlag, Mainz, 1963, pp. 11-24.

The author makes the point that the distinction between a

philosophical ethic, a philosophy of morality, which is other than a "practical" ethic, is not at all self-evident. The question reported in HB"When will you write an ethic ?" is taken up within this framework.

71.   GAMBRA, R. "Posibilidades éticas en el existencialismo". *Revista de filosofía,* 11 (1952), 401-442.

This article deals almost exclusively with Sartre; yet, H's description of inauthentic existence is stressed as a life reduced to instances without presence. No development is had and no reference beyond SZ.

72.   GONDA, J. "Wereld en hemel in de Veda". *Tijdschrift voor filosofie,* 28 (1966), 227-63.

Though no mention is had of Heidegger, this most interesting work on the oriental notion of "Lucus-Locus" suggests to us a crux-passage from HB. Cf. above page 49 for our reasons.

73a.   GRENE, Marjorie. *Martin Heidegger* (Studies in Modern European Literature and Thought). Hillary House, New York, 1957, 128 pp.

More of journalistic than of philosophic interest, the freedom of movement in this work may be stimulating esp. to those with little formal philosophical reflection. For our purpose, at least, it is of no value. — We include it only because of our effort to be more thorough in the limited literature in English.

73b.   *Dreadful Freedom. A Critique of Existentialism.* University of Chicago Press, 1948 (And: Cambridge University Press, London), 149pp. [Also, reissued as *Introduction to Existentialism,* Chicago, 1959].

In a major portion of this book, there is a free weaving in and out of Sartre and Heidegger; though we find no particular light on the subject, we may perhaps savour the A's approach: "But what Sartre and Heidegger profess is the exact contrary of that Kantian restriction; that in dealing with things as they seem to us we are dealing with them as they are. Here, I must humbly confess, I simply cannot follow them, unless in the spirit in which one follows Alice down the rabbit-hole".

74. HARRIES, Karsten. "Heidegger's Conception of the Holy". *The Personalist* (Los Angeles), 47 (1966), 169-184.

Of particular interest is the opinion that H's ontological difference seems to deny mediation without which ethics is impossible. Though a provoking article, with some sharp insight, it is marked with undue confusion and oversimplification.

75. HEISE, Wolfgang. *Aufbruch in die Illusion. Zur Kritik der bürgerlichen Philosophie in Deutschland.* Veb Deutscher Verlag der Wissenschaften, Berlin, 1964. 498 pp.

Though at once more serious and more vituperative, this book follows the same line as no. 62. Cf. pp. 253-4, 364.

76. HINNERS, Richard. "The Freedom and Finiteness of Existence in Heidegger". *New Scholasticism*, 33 (1959), 32-48.

The A sets up the question in reference to Sartre and the standard HB reference but then moves on to SZ and WG to end his wanderings by invoking HB. A needless journey.

77. HOLLENBACH, Johannes-M. *Sein und Gewissen. Über den Ursprung der Gewissensregung. Eine Begegnung zwischen Martin Heidegger und thomistischer Philosophie.* Grimm, Verlag für Kunst und Wissenschaft, Baden-Baden, 1954, 373 pp.

For our purpose, one should note the A's treatment of the project character of comprehension ("der Entwurfcharakter des Verstehens"). Project is neither present-ative nor a production of subjectivity; it *is* "der ekstatische Bezug zur Lichtung" of HB, 17 explained in terms of freedom (as in WW).

78. KUSCHBERT-TÖLLE, Helga. "Heideggers Ansatz beim grieschen Seinsverständnis als Grundstruktur seines Denkens". *Philosophisches Jahrbuch,* 79 (1962), 138-146.

This study on the nature of thought [Denken, Dichten, andenkendes Denken: eigentliche Entsprechung] stresses its "structure", its realization through struggle (phýsis, lógos) and through the *Gestalt* concretizing and hiding Being as well as man, the "shepherd", with the quest of standing in authentic correspondence. This "heideggerian" study, which by no means merely mouthes H, is pertinent since humanism's essence belongs to this type of thinking.

79. LANDMANN, Michael. *Philosophische Anthropologie. Menschliche Selbstdeutung in Geschichte und Gegenwart.* 2., durchgesehene Aufl. Sammlung Göschen Bd 156/156a. Walter de Gruyter & Co., Berlin, 1964. 223 pp.

It is clearly of some interest to see how H is situated within a survey of the entire field of anthropology, a task made easy by this book's index. The A is definitely most unsympathetic (53); one should note the relationship drawn with Dilthey.

80. LEYVRAZ, Jean-Pierre. "Le moment du choix chez Heidegger". *Studia Philosophica* (Basel), 26 (1966), 139-58.

This article can be read most profitably as a complement to the question we formulated on HB: it is essential to know whether H's thought really allows for a real encounter. The question can be put in terms of the finite-infinite and the indefinite; the field of choice as Sein's or Dasein's, etc.

81.   MARCEL, Gabriel. *L'Homme problématique.* Aubier, Paris, 1955. 187 pp.

Within the personal thought of this remarkable philosopher, one finds richly meaningful references to H and HB precisely where the A deals with a most fundamental aspect of the question of "values" and man as the "shepherd of Being" (48-51). On "humanisation", cf. 50-58.

82.   MOSER, Simon. *Metaphysik einst und jetzt. Kritische Untersuchungen zu Begriff und Ansatz der Ontologie.* Walter de Gruyter & Co., Berlin, 1958. 294 pp.

Within the very long chapter on H, one finds (103-116) an exposition of HB in terms of the perennial question of the relation beings-Being opening up on the God-question. Though our own question is not treated, it is often complemented, e.g., "...in die Nähe des Nächsten" [103] is interpreted as an "Überplatonismus von Seinsglaube und Seinshoffnung". Good questions are asked, though occasionally coming in unannounced out of the cold of scholasticism. This defect is made up by the general sweep of the book covering a central question (phýsis, Seiendes, Sein und Technik) throughout Western philosophy by concentrating on a few authors.

83.   MÜLLER-LAUTER, Wolfgang. *Möglichkeit und Wirklichkeit bei Martin Heidegger.* Walter de Gruyter & Co., Berlin, 1960. 107 pp.

Beginning with an analysis of SZ's "meaning of possibility as existential within the fundamental analysis of Dasein" (4), this book ends (104-5) with an essential part of the HB-question: the relationship between "Mensch", "Dasein" and "Da-sein" according to which are interpreted HB, 72 ("Kehre") and 69 (man as the "Da") — interesting esp. as a straightforward exposition of the problematic's continuity.

84. Noller, Gerhard. *Sein und Existenz. Die Überwindung des Subjekt-Objektschemas in der Philosophie Heideggers und in der Theologie der Entmythologisierung.* Chr. Kaiser Verlag, München, 1962. 166 pp.

Of some interest would be the A's treatment (59) of HB, 21f (sc., man is not merely one who has the capacity of language but language is the house which he inhabits) in conjunction with language as a structure which is developed from the well-known and very difficult passages of SZ, 158, 163, without, however, an attempt at further clarification (e.g., through the use of ID). But, then, inspite of its title, this work does not contribute much.

85. Ott, Heinrich. *Denken und Sein. Der Weg Martin Heideggers und der Weg der Theologie.* Evangelischer Verlag Zollikon, 1959. 226 pp.

Though there is only a brief comment on humanism and subjectivism according to PW, 49, it has a prophetic ring: precisely in the middle of the book (117), one section ends with the notion of humanism and the end of metaphysics, the next begins with Nietzsche's "God-is-dead".

86. Pugliese, Orlando. *Vermittlung und Kehre. Grundzüge des Geschichtsdenkens bei Martin Heidegger.* "Symposion". Verlag Karl Alber Freiburg/München, 1965. 226 pp.

In this meticulously detailed work, unified by the "and" of Being *and* Time as well as Time *and* Being, one sees that the type of thinking in question in HB is that very one described as an attempt, a preparation, as road-markers ("Wegzeichen eines Weges", 81), whose source is a universal fundamental experience: "Die Erschütterung alles Seienden und die Heimatlosigkeit des Menschen", which is above all expressed by HB [91].

87. ROBERTS, David E. *Existentialism and Religious Belief*. A Galaxy Book. Oxford University Press, New York, 1959.

In this remarkable survey, one finds H's emphasis on mystery as an approach underscoring anti-anthropomorphism which the A links (172) with the tradition of the "via negativa" in reference specifically to HB, 76. The richness of the context cannot help but complement the HB-question.

88. ROESSINGH, K.H. *Martin Heidegger als godsdienstwijsgeer*. Van Gorcum, Assen, 1956. 240 pp.

The A brings out the periods of H's thought among which the "holy" is evidently the A's principal interest; however, an analysis of the "epochal" is wanting. Of special interest, nevertheless, is how man realizes himself in time; this is examined from HB as being fundamentally a polarity of struggle, one which is grounded in Being itself (191ff).

89. ROSSI, Guido. "Existenzialismo e Cristianesimo". *Sapienza* (Bologna), 2 (1949), 219-32.

We include this article as a fine example of a limit-case. One is simply stupified by the rigid, rationalistic misreading of Kierkegaard, Heidegger, Jaspers and Marcel. The Dasein of SZ is a misconception of its simplest statements; a passion for clear thought reduces all else to intuitive illusions — an exercise in non-dialogue.

90. RÜEGG, W. "Humanismus". In: *Die Religion in Geschichte und Gegenwart*. JCB Mohr, Tübingen, 1959 [cf. no. 60, *supra*], 3. Bd., 481.

The value of this article rests at once on the incisiveness of its statement on H's "humanism of Being" and on its immediate setting: the statement is preceeded by Sartre's humanism with reference to Marxist and Catholic critics, it is followed by the "humanism of dialectical theology".

91. Ryffel, H. "Zu den neuen Veröffentlichungen von M. Heidegger". *Studia Philosophica* (Basel), 15 (1955) 176-202.

The A attacks H for his "nationalism" whose traces remain in HB and later works where it has been merely transformed by a "neutralized" language. When one recalls the hermeneutical problem of how much of an author's known lived content should be carried over into one's reading, one should at least hesitate to discard the question of nationalism by means of a simplistic dichotomy.

92. Schulz, Walter. "Über den philosophiegeschichtlichen Ort Martin Heideggers". *Philosophische Rundschau*, 1 (1953/54), 65-93; 211-232.

The importance of this article is such that, though it does not take up our question, it's silence appears to us as a true interpretation. For what is the significance of the fact that in treating extensively of "place", "Dasein" and "language" the A, even when dealing with HB, can pass over in silence "man", "humanism" and "ethics" ?

93. Strolz, Walter. *Der vergessene Ursprung. Das moderne Weltbild, die neuzeitliche Denkbewegung und die Geschichtlichkeit des Menschen.* Herder, Basel-Freiburg-Wien, 1959, 170 pp.

Since the HB-question touches philosophical thought in its very relation with scientific thinking, this book can be usefully complementary, esp. 66-67, and passim — there being many more reference to H than the A gives in his index.

94a. Waelhens, Alphonse de. *Phénoménologie et vérité. Essai sur l'évolution de l'idée de vérité chez Husserl et Heidegger.* P U F, Paris, 1953. 167 pp.

The A, one of the most competent of commentators, does not explicitate at length our question but the few allusions are always incisive. In this book, HB stands in the light of "truth" (as in PW) in view of "work" (as in HW) and the work of art (and "thought as originally poetry and language"). This can easily be read in terms of humanism and in order to balance, for example, Fürstenau's (no. 24) analysis of work of art and to put into context Schwan's (no. 52) "work of truth". Cf. esp. 87, 150, 152-54, the latter takes up HB's idea of the history of Being as determining every human condition and situation as a more adequate expression for "human nature".

94b.   "HEIDEGGER, Platon et l'humanisme". *Revue philosophique de Louvain*, 46 (1948), 490-96.

The early date of this article limits its scope to a clearly focused summary of PW and HB. H's intention is spelled out from the text without needless distraction: H considers himself the defender of the only true "humanism" in that he accords to man his priviledged position, his philosophy alone could found an authentic ethic. — Anyone who would wish to claim that H is consciously anti-humanistic, or better "anti-human", should at least reconsider the clear line of this summary.

95.   WEISCHEDEL, W. "Weg und Irrweg im abendländischen Denken". *Zeitschrift für philosophische Forschung*, 7 (1953), 3-19.

There are two basic approaches — or better "Gänge der Auslegung" —: Hegel and Plato (Augustine, Descartes), a third way, keeping both in mind, is found in HW and esp. HB whose *via media* is set forth as the task. This line-up makes for provocative reading when one asks what H might mean by a "new humanism".

CORRELATION OF TEXTS

HB/PW

5/53-4
6/54-6
7/56-7
8/57-9
9/59-60
10/60-2
11/62-3
12/63-5
13/65-7
14/67-8
15/68-70
16/70-71
17/71-3
18/73-4
19/74-6
20/76-7
21/77-9
22/79-80
23/80-2
24/82-3
25/83-5

HB/PW

26/85-7
27/87-8
28/88-90
29/90-1
30/91-3
31/93-4
32/94-6
33/96-7
34/97-9
35/99-101
36/101-02
37/102-04
38/104-05
39/105-07
40/107-08
41/108-10
42/110-11
43/111-13
44/113-15
45/115-16
46/116-18
47/118-19

TABLE OF CONTENTS

Preface 5

I Introduction 7

II A Reading of the Letter 23

   A Note on the English Translation 61

III The Interpretations of the Letter 65

IV Critical Bibliography 83

   Complementary Bibliography 127

   Correlation of Texts 139